To my Dearest Friend and
Inspiration
      Love always—

        Amy

HELEN KELLEY'S

JOY OF
Quilting

HELEN KELLEY'S

JOY OF
Quilting

More Wit and Wisdom from America's
Most Popular Quilting Columnist

whitecap

DEDICATION
to quilters everywhere

CONTENTS

PREFACE   10

CHAPTER 1: *'Round the Quilt Frame*

Blessed Endurance   18

To Sleep: Perchance to Dream   20

Oh, Baby, Look at Me Now!   23

Pseudo Suits Me   26

Say It Loud and Clear   30

Feeling Good   33

I Come With Attachments   36

Mixed Blessings   42

Touch-Me-Not   45

Sweet Mystery   48

CHAPTER 2: *Glory Be!*

On Necessity and Invention   54

Fitting and Proper   56

The Name's the Game   59

It's Always an Adventure   62

Another Slant   65

Siren Song   68

Hind Sight	71
Thanks, I Needed That!	74
Security Blanket	78
All That's Gold Does Not Glitter	81
All Right, Sew What?	83

CHAPTER 3: *Tying Up Loose Ends*

Setting Priorities	88
Hip! Hip! Hooray!	90
It's How You Play the Game	93
My Life Doesn't Add Up	96
Wonder Woman vs. the World	98
The State of Civilization	100
Up to My Neck in Deep Water	103
Showers of Blessings	106
Thread Sales in the Sunset	109
No Strings Attached	111
A Little Something Worth Mentioning. . .	113
Craziness	116

CHAPTER 4: *Words By Which to Sew a Stitch*

Words to Live By	122
My Stars!	124
Sea Sighs	127
Thursday's Child	129
Bittersweet	132
Quoth the Raven	136
A Fable	139
My Refuge, and My Strength	141
My Heart Leaps Up	143
Following the Thread of the Story	145
Eensy Weensy Spider	148

CHAPTER 5: *Family Matters*

The Great Cover-Up	154
Measure for Measure	157
"M"	163
Bye Baby Bunting	167
There Is a Season	170
My Luv Is Not a Red, Red Quilt	172

Baby, Take a Bow! 175

Sitting Pretty 177

Plying My Trade 180

Chapter 6: *A Stitch in Time*

Facing the New Year 186

Stormy Weather 189

Am I Blue? 191

Cure for a Common Cold 194

Grandma's Flower Garden, Kinda 197

How Does Your Garden Grow? 205

As Ye Sow, So Shall Ye Sew 207

Reconsidering the Lilies 210

The Winds of Was 213

I Am Venus 217

Tenderfoot 221

IMAGINE THIS—A BEAUTY queen stands on the stage in the glow of the footlights in her teeny-tiny bathing suit and her royal sash. The contest judge asks her, "And what would you like to do with your life?" The fantasy queen replies, "I would like to bring about world peace."

Well, I am no beauty queen, but I can tell you how I would do this. The recipe for world peace is to bring all of the international leaders together around a quilt frame. This suggestion does not sound ridiculous to anyone who has ever sat side-by-side and hip-to-hip with creative quilters, working in harmony with one another to produce something beautiful. While sitting around that quilt frame, the world leaders could sort out the troublemakers, settle international disputes, and put a whole new face on the art of cooperation and candor and creativity. How many times have you read about something or someone gone wrong, and heard a listener comment, "Well, it couldn't have been a quilter who did that." From quilters you can expect integrity and generosity.

I quilt because I like to be with quilters. It's true that I love to feel fabric and that I am probably in the running for the title of World's Most Compulsive, Every-Day, All-Day Maker of Quilts, but it's the people I meet who are the real reason why I do this quilt-thing. On most days, I work alone in my workroom. I listen to the radio while I squint at fabric to determine which colors blend and what colors make my quilt sparkle. I cut fabric. Recently, I expanded my cutting table area to the size of an entire 30x60-inch office table by adding a gigantic cutting mat; now I have a huge area where I can measure and cut and stack up my patchwork pieces to my heart's content. I sew. My sewing machine is precious to me and I treat it kindly, dusting and oiling and pampering it to keep it healthy and happy. I iron. I don't make excuses anymore for my beloved, tatty ironing board that stands permanently in the center of all this disarray, ready at a moment's notice for the gentle touch of my iron, pressing my quilt blocks smooth and flat.

I know that there are some people who actually fold up their ironing boards and put them away out of sight when they are not using them. These same people dust and vacuum their workrooms, fold their neatly cut and trimmed leftover fabrics into color rainbows that shine through the clear plastic sides of their containers. Their work spaces are a triumph, indeed. My work space is not. It is home to my cutting board and sewing machine and ironing board, and I like to have them always ready for me. I tell you this because I want you to understand that making quilts truly is a passion for me, but it is not my primary passion. My primary passion is quilters themselves.

I work in a solitary manner, and periodically I realize that I miss the company of other quilters, so I go to a quilt store, or to a guild meeting, or gather with friends for coffee, and I listen to them talk. Their enthusiasm refuels me. Quilters are exciting people. Their passion is infectious. They do for me exactly what a support group should do: they support and renew me.

Then, I go back to my quiet work in the clutter of my room, refreshed. My mind whirls with the energy I have absorbed from my friends, and then, I think. I think about quilters and I think about quilts, old and new, theirs and mine. I think about the challenges and the triumphs that every quilt represents and the endurance and the love of the people who have made them, and as I think, stories emerge. My stories are about these people, all of whom I cherish.

Last night was one of those times when I felt that I needed another quilter, and so I had dinner with a friend. She gave me a present—four large boxes of quilting rubble, things that she had rooted out of her mother's workroom when she was rearranging her own life after her mother's passing. I have spent the morning sorting through antique quilt tops and pieces of fabric folded into kaleidoscopic piles, ready to make star quilts. There is a collection of patterns, some whose envelopes have never even been opened. There are antique lace hankies and embroidered doilies, quilted pot holders and tools. And all of these things tell me a story about this quiltmaker who had treasured them.

It is obvious that she was a shopper. She bought these things with uncontrolled enthusiasm. For instance, there are a dozen metal finger protectors to be used on the forefinger of the vulnerable hand held beneath the fame

– – – –

when hand quilting. I am sure she did not have a dozen fingers. In the excitement of shopping, she must have bought them as gifts for her fellow quilters. She was a generous woman with a long list of friends.

She was an insightful woman. I concluded this from the big pile of old quilt blocks and the scraps and pieces that she had rescued from antique stores. She must have quivered with excitement when she discovered these treasures. They surely spoke to her, hinting to her of the lives of the women before her who had created them. She was a thrifty person and a saver, salvaging her leavings and leftovers to be recycled in future quilts.

In other words, this woman was a typical quilter. She was generous, insightful, thrifty, and, oh my, how she did love to shop! Now I am the keeper of her treasury. I will send off her antique blocks and tops to our local quilt history project so that members can learn about old fabrics and the quilters who used them. I will donate the box of folded fabrics to a church group to be used to create comforts for their mission project. I will offer the delicate hankerchiefs and hand-embroidered doilies to my quilt group to sell in their annual garage sale, a fundraising event for the scholarship fund. In this way, my friend's bounty will go on as it should, extending her mother's generosity.

Back in my own little world, my workroom floor is covered with threads and quilt batt fuzz and shreds of fabric. It is a mess and it is exactly the way I like it. I've had a wonderful idea. The mailperson brought me a box

- - - -

this morning, and inside, I found a collection of very old table linen. My sister had found the placemats that my mother used for us on special occasions. They are linen rectangles with silk-screened illustrations drawn by Tony Sarg, a book illustrator and puppet-maker during the 1920s and 30s. His pictures are colorful renditions of Bavarian folk art, with all its flowers and quaint flourishes. I have memories of birthday parties where these placemats decorated the table. Certainly they are too precious to use for eating on now.

So, what to do with them? Why not make memories with them for my own daughters? I will sew wall hangings. Each will be an imaginary table with a place mat on the top and bottom and a bowl of three-dimensional fabric flowers in the center. I will embellish them with fabric silverware and call each quilted hanging "Dinner with Grandmother." My mind began to effervesce as the vision took hold. I didn't even stop to toss the package wrappings into the trash. I pulled out fabric from my stash and piled it on the floor. I dipped into bins of material and dug into caches at the back of my closet. I was swept up with the excitement.

Then, I sorted and cut out pieces, sewed them together, and surrounded them with walnut-colored fabric just the color of my mother's dining room table. Here and now, these little quilts are happening, just as I envisioned them. Music is playing on the radio. My heart is racing. I dash between the cutting board, the ironing board, and my sewing machine, churning out flower pieces

– – – –

before stitching them into quilt units and finally join-ing them together to make my wall-hangings. This is exactly what making a quilt should be like. I am practi-cally vibrating with the excitement, and when I grow weary from all of this frantic activity, I will call my best quilt friend to come over for coffee so that I can tell her all about this. And that is the key to my quilting—shar-ing the delight. I must show these things to my friend and we will admire them together.

That is really what this book is about—sharing my everyday quilting experiences, both good and bad, with other quilters and quilt lovers. Every day I quilt a bit. Every day of my life brings new challenges. Every day brings something that delights me and makes me laugh. I freely admit to cutting fabric wrong and dis-covering bleeding materials in my finished quilts when I have been too lazy to wash and prepare my fabrics properly before I sewed them. Some people are em-barrassed to admit their mistakes and frustrations, but I am a woman without shame. These stories about my triumphs and tragedies are real, and I share them with you because it is always comforting to find someone who has made the same hasty blunders that you have. These stories are my own contribution to that univer-sal "quilter's support group" that I talked about ear-lier. I hope you enjoy them!

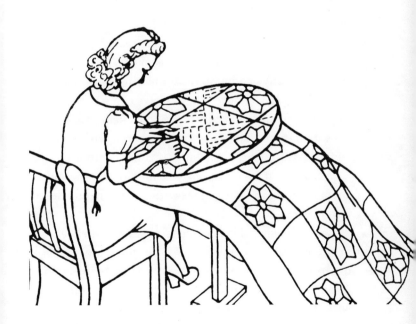

BLESSED ENDURANCE

QUILTERS ARE A HARDY BREED OF HUMAN. THEY ENDURE! Think of that frontier woman peering out of her tiny window, if she had one, at the eternal snow—waiting, waiting for the road to be opened, for the spring, for the time for the quilt frame to be put out, and for her neighbors to come to quilt. Have you ever been in one of those tiny log cabins and marveled at the survival of those women through the winters?

Think of today's quilters, sitting at their frames, fingers worn through as they finish the last row of quilting on This Quilt and already the next two quilts shaped and stitched in their minds. Think of how the worst winter days always come on quilt-meeting days, and yet, incredibly, they endure. They always come to the meetings. They come wind-tossed, red-cheeked, jittery from cars dancing on ice. They come covered with snow or wet with rain. They come laughing and excited.

What is that special quality about quilters that takes them through the hard times with optimism and determination?

Recently when I was discussing a quilt theft with a group of quilters, one said, "It couldn't have been a quilter who took it!" She was acknowledging that quilters are special people. I used to think that quilting—with its requirements for planning ahead and demands of precision—created these people. I have changed my

- - - -

mind. Perhaps special people create quilts. They share a love of beautiful things, a pleasure in each other, and, yes, endurance. The true quilter does not rush home from the grocery store with a magazine that tells her how to cut, stitch, and produce a coverlet in an evening. The joy of the true quilter is in the planning, the plotting, and the searching of fabric stores. It is in the sketching, stitching, and savoring. Every planned new quilt is a vision.

Maybe it doesn't matter which comes first, the quilt or the quilter. Maybe what matters is the special qualities of quilters. Maybe what matters is that in spite of weather, work, or worry, every quilter endures and has a dream.

TO SLEEP: PERCHANCE TO DREAM

THERE IS A CHILD'S STORY ABOUT A MYTHICAL CHARACTER named Ole Luk Oye (the Sandman). He comes to sit on your bed at night and holds an umbrella over you. The umbrella is filled with wondrous dreams. Why is it that Ole Luk Oye is never there when I need him?

I'm just home from one of our modern "gathering of the clans," that giant quilting bee, a quilt symposium. I was so excited before I ever left home that I was tired when I arrived. From the moment I saw that first quilted vest and said, "Hi, you're a quilter, I bet!" I never stopped fizzling like a glass of ginger ale.

The quiltmakers congregated. They formed in clumps around the coffee pots, in snack bars, at the lectures, and most particularly in the rooms at night, sometimes *all* night. They produced marvels from their trash-bag bundles, and everyone fingered. Everyone examined and admired.

At the quilt-historians' meeting, the participants were researchers. They had impeccable and impressive reputations. They had collections of everything–literature, fabrics, pictures, old and new quilts, and notes, notes, notes. Individually their knowledge was amazing. Collectively they boggled the mind. The marvelous thing was their generosity: they wanted to know how they could help each other.

The quilt merchants sat behind their heaped-up tables. The patterns were tempting, the fabric dazzling. The only thing that saved me from bankruptcy was the quantity available. I could never have chosen. I wouldn't have known where to begin to choose. One store owner told me that to save herself from decision making, she takes home a length of everything she has in her store. Can you imagine what her fabric closet must look like? There were new kinds of plastic, cutting boards, graph paper. Only creative quilters could have dreamed up the innovations that tempted me.

The quilt teachers were efficient and organized. They were enthusiastic, warm, and prepared to tantalize us into stretching our minds and imaginations. Not all of the teachers stood in front of the class, I discovered. The quilter sitting next to me with another mind, another background, another impetus sometimes had wonderfully wise things to say.

No wonder I couldn't get to sleep after splashing all day in that great big bowl of quilt-borsch. I went to bed at a decent time. It was about midnight. I lay in bed and flipped back to front and back again. I wiggled down. I wriggled back up. I threw back the covers. The room seemed warm. I got up and checked the air conditioner. Now the room seemed cold. I got up and checked the thermostat. My roommate was rolling around. At one point, I got up in the dark to examine the treasures I had bought during the day. My roommate got up, and in the blackness she stumbled and fell across the end of her bed. Together we leaned on the windowsill and admired the lighted skyline. We giggled. We laughed. Sometime between three and three-thirty Ole Luk Oye showed up. He put up his umbrella. At last we dreamed. Do you know, we dreamed of quilts.

– – – –

OH, BABY, LOOK AT ME NOW!

LOOK AT ME! I CAN'T BELIEVE THAT I'M SUCH A BIG BABY. My behavior embarrasses me. Let me tell you my story.

Ordinarily, I am about the healthiest person alive. Except for the occasional headache, I'm rarely sick. When I woke this morning, I discovered that I could not move my body. With the slightest movement, a pain shot across my lower back, through my hip, and down my leg. I tried to turn over. "Oh, wowowowow!" I yelled. Bill put his head in the bedroom door to see what was happening. I tried again. "Owow!" Another searing pain shot down my back. Gently, he put his arms around me, and supporting my hip, he eased my body over the edge of the bed. This maneuver was accompanied by a great deal more wowing. Somehow, yesterday, I had sprung my back. Maybe I did it when I lifted fabric boxes down from the closet shelf. Maybe I did it when I crawled on the floor to baste my new quilt. I have no memory of the "when," only the "what"—this crippling soreness.

That day, I minced around the house, moaning and groaning and inventing some exquisite sighs. Fortunately, opening mail and pushing microwave buttons take very little physical exertion. "My pain" was a wonderful excuse to avoid the chores I would rather not do, such as bedmaking, floor-sweeping, or sorting and folding laundry.

– – – –

That was quilt guild meeting night. I went. I would have been more comfortable moping at home, enthroned in front of the TV with the heating pad cradled against my backside, but a friend called when she heard that I was crippled. She came round to pick me up and drive me to the meeting hall. I was armed with a soft, fat cushion to pad the rigid, metal folding chair. I patted the pillow in place, sat down on it, and sighed, audibly.

It was a great meeting! The speaker was a quilter I had wanted to hear for several years. She had brought interesting quilts, made by her family of quilters, and she laced her talk with anecdotes. I learned a lot.

There is another reason why attending that guild meeting was especially significant for me. As I sat there padded and cushioned and feeling sorry for myself, I looked around me. I studied the other quilters, some I have known for years, and realized that, obviously, I have taken these women for granted. Some are young and energetic, filled with vibrancy. Others are less supple. They have canes to help them walk. Some have arthritic hands, and they have had to devise new ways to approach their lives. Some have deteriorating eyesight and wear strong glasses. Some live with daily discomfort. These people don't heap their difficulties, their aches and pains onto their friends' shoulders. They don't moan and groan. They don't mince about. They do not sigh. They deal with their challenges in a quiet, determined, and cheerful manner.

– – – –

During the show-and-tell section of our meeting, a parade of quilters crossed the stage. Each held up a quilt and told of the joy of making that quilt, of the planning, the stitching, the using, the gifting, and the sharing. I was ashamed of myself as I watched them. My own backache was temporary, a brief discomfort, and I was making a dramatic display.

Therefore, I dedicate these thoughts to all quilters, but especially to those who live the days of their lives with disabilities. For those people who have found ways to be creative in spite of their discomfort, who make beautiful quilts, with bent hands or with bent eyesight, my admiration is unbounded.

I expect that tomorrow when I wake. I shall leap out of bed free of pain, and I shall hurtle through the day as I have always done before. The difference, tomorrow, will be that I will do it with gratitude. If I were Wordsworth, I would write this tribute with rhyming words and rollicking meter. If I were Beethoven, I would compose an *Ode to Joy,* but I am not a great poet or a celebrated musician. I am me, a quilter. So, for these remarkable people that I know, I write this, my own, personal tribute to them, my *Hallelujah Chorus.*

- - - -

PSEUDO SUITS ME

I AM NOT A SOCIOLOGIST, BUT I HAVE NOTICED THE scientific jargon used to describe society. If one reads the Sunday paper or the *Reader's Digest* even casually, one is likely to pick up some of the "in" words and, by using them, appear to talk knowledgeably on sociological subjects.

Quilters, it would appear, have become a subculture of their own. We have grown in a few short years into a very distinct group that has developed its own set of norms. I tend to be a Rebel, and my response to Dos and Don'ts (or more strongly, Musts and Must Nots) is "Who says?" I think it behooves us, since we are hereby dipping into scientific waters, to take a good look at ourselves and consider our norms.

Some of these are common sense. Some of them deal with good manners, like saying "please" and "thank you." They also include offering another quilter a needle when hers has disappeared into the rug and not taking the last party mint on the tea table. Norms indicate that when a woman shows you her finished quilt, she should not be asked why in the world she chose *that* color. They include arriving on time at quilt meetings, not talking to your neighbor in audible tones while the speaker is making her presentation, nor snoozing with your mouth open during the slides. There are, after all, certain civilized requirements set forth for us.

– – – –

Some of these norms make sense because things look better when we comply with them. We make our quilts so that they hang straight against the wall or lie smoothly on the bed. We should make our points meet neatly. We should remove marking lines somehow if we can only find a good solution to the removal problem short of disintegration of the fabric.

Then we get into a gray area. These are norms that have been set forth by somebody and which have nothing to do with beauty or practicality. And that is what cultures do, set up norms that only those within the culture can understand and appreciate (or not appreciate). Quilters have lots of those.

Every time we put a quilt in a quilt show they surface. Sometimes these norms become a point of contention between judges. Always they are disputed among the participants. Now, all of the quilt show judges out there are going to throw up their hands in despair. They do, after all, have to have some sort of measuring stick, and if you and I are going to enter quilt shows, I guess we have to play their game. That means abiding by their norms. Yet, I still have a few healthy questions. Where did these rules come from? Who made them up?

WHO SAYS...

* that corners must be mitered unless you are Amish, and then you are allowed to butt them?

* that bindings must be hand-stitched in place unless you happen to be a Mennonite lady and then you are permitted to machine them?

* that you must quilt geometric pieces with straight-line patterns and graceful pieces with soft flowers and feathers, even if you have a better, more wonderful design in your mind?

* that you must quilt right beside the seam? Or, on the other hand, who says that you must quilt exactly ¼" from the edges?

* that you must always quilt with white thread? Or with colored matching thread? Or that you may not use a variety of colored threads all in the same piece?

* that you should not bring your back to the front or your front to the back when finishing if you anchor your batting inside to fill all the way to the edges?

* that edges must be bound with bias? Or with straight-grain strips?

* that the colors you choose are not appropriate when they are appropriate for you?

– – – –

All of this goes to say that not everybody is going to like every quilt. Of course not! Somebodies have set up these norms and obviously even somebodies don't always agree. Nevertheless, if we want to get along in this quilting society, we have to conform to the norms. We have to acknowledge that there are preferable ways of doing things.

When we come to a red traffic light, we stop, even when there is no other traffic and no policeman in sight. There are some things that society requires of us to ensure order, things that we as people of integrity respect. When we make our quilts, there are some standards that have been set for us, and when you survey the products of our quilting society, our spectacular quilts with their colors flowing across the surface, dipping and fluffing gracefully, maybe there is something to this business of setting guidelines, something about ensuring order. Ours is a society that is productive. It is progressive. It is certainly civilized. and it certainly does produce beautiful quilts.

SAY IT LOUD AND CLEAR

BILL IS STANDING OUTSIDE, SHADING HIS EYES AND staring up at our chimney. Our house was built before World War II, and the chimney is made of cement bricks. The bricks are spalling—flaking and crumbling.

Once back inside, Bill asks, "What if we rebuild the chimney, and we discover damage under the adjoining roof? What if there is no damage, but the newer building codes require updating the structure? Can we put off the repair for another year?"

I'm not the person to ask. I wouldn't know a spall from a spool. No, I take that back . . . I would know a spool. "Why," I ask, "don't you go about this in the same way I solve quilting problems? You need somebody with building experience who won't be offended if you don't take his suggestions. A chimney conversation might shed some light on the problem."

I have a very good friend to whom I talk about my quilting. When I have wrestled with a problem until I am upset, I scoop my quilting project into my arms and go to see her. I head straight for her living room and spread my quilt top out on her carpet. "I wrestled with this late into the night yesterday, then went to bed and dreamed about it. This morning, I wasn't any closer to figuring out what's wrong with it. I made it exactly like I planned it, and it's wrong, wrong, wrong."

- - - -

"Hm!" says Norma, looking over my shoulder. "Needs yellow."

"Any more yellow and it will look like a fruit basket," I pout.

"Why don't you move that cluster of buildings just a smidgen?"

"I can't move anything," I wail. "It's all sewn into place."

"How about a line of embroidery to highlight that hill?"

"No! This quilt is not supposed to have embroidery!" I protest.

Suddenly, "I know," I crow. "I'll add a tiny, olive-colored tree to the skyline. That'll shift the balance and give it the breath of life."

"Have a cup of coffee," says Norma.

Talking with my friend unlocks my brain and frees it. I think it's because I have to sort my thoughts, put them in order, and then hear the problem voiced aloud, listening to it play against my ears. When I talk to wonderful, understanding Norma, I come back to my workroom refreshed and with a new direction.

I have a surrogate friend to talk aloud to when I am alone in my workroom, a sort of second-best Norma, but it seems to work. I talk to myself. Myself and I get very excited when we discuss deep questions, such as which shade of red nestles best beside a teal-colored fabric wedge. The key word here is "aloud." I speak, I listen, and I answer myself, and that verbal exchange unlocks the wheels and gears in my head, and once they are moving and meshing, the solutions seem to come. I think everybody needs somebody to talk aloud with, whether it's an alter ego or, best of all, a knowledgeable friend.

So, perhaps this is the solution to our chimney problem. Bill needs to tell his thoughts and worries to another person, who knows construction language, who will offer suggestions, and free Bill's mind to problem-solve. Just as I go to another quilter to needle my mind, so Bill must find himself someone to help him frame his thoughts and hammer out his solution.

FEELING GOOD

HAS ANYONE EVER ASKED YOU A QUESTION THAT LEFT you so speechless, so shocked and surprised that you couldn't frame a reply? I was talking to a lady. She was a very nice lady, someone I had never met before. We made light conversation. We asked each other the usual questions, like, "What do you do?"

"I'm a quiltmaker," I told her.

There was a long, uneasy pause as the lady tried to sort this out in her mind. It was as if I had said that I raise barracudas or fly stunt planes. Obviously, making quilts was a new thought to her. She was groping for a polite reply.

"I suppose you have lots of quilts?" she asked.

"Oh, yes, lots of them," I said. "I always have one in the making and one in my head."

There was another uneasy pause. After another silence, she asked, "What do you do with them?"

"I, well, I...you know, I...I..."

What do I do with my quilts? It was as if the lady had asked me what I do with my children. What do I do with my quilts? I told the nice lady something that I thought she could understand. I told her that I have a few on my beds, and that occasionally, I give one of my quilts as a gift. Sometimes, I wrap a grandchild in one for a nap. I may snuggle under one while I watch TV. I may hang one on my wall to delight me each time I pass it. I did not

– – – –

add that I have lots of quilts on my shelves that I count, talk to, and fold and refold. She would not have understood that I like to feel my quilts.

When I make a quilt, I find joy in puzzling out the colors and the design. I love to sort the fabrics, to cut and stack then, to stitch them together so that they lie smooth and flat and the hues melt into each other, piece by piece until the patterns take shape and bloom. The most pleasure in all those fabrics, though, is that I like the feel of them as I work.

The rhythm of quilting sings to me. It is like a sedative, like the gentle rocking of a drifting boat as it nestles in the water. My hands move across the face of the quilt, stitching, tacking down the puffs and the billows, etching the pattern, lifting it into a third dimension. The softness is a silent pleasure. The feel is satisfying.

When I finish my quilt. I lay it out on the bed or hang it high on my wall, and I run my hands across the surface. I smooth it and pat it down. I reassure it. There is a shiver of pleasure that runs through me when I see my quilt finished and soft and gentle and touchable. The nice lady would not have understood all of this.

We, as quilters, gather in guilds each month to meet people who all speak our language and experience the same love. I do not need to explain to each of you that I love to feel my quilts. You know what I mean. As quilters, we sew a variety of quilts. We may make quilted toaster covers or dog blankets. We may make baby buntings or

– – – –

fashionable vests or draft stoppers for our doors. We may make stuffed bears and rabbits wearing patchwork dresses or elegant pillows, dormitory comforters, or commodious tote bags. We may make big, soft quilts or small wall hangings. Whatever we make, we all do the same things—sorting, cutting, stitching, and feeling.

A person may read home-decorating magazines or visit antique stores to admire quilts, but until he or she has actually sewn pieces of fabric together and stitched them into a quilt, until that person has touched and felt them, handled them and loved them, that person cannot understand the mystery of quiltmaking. Admire them? Oh, certainly. That's easy. Quilts are beautiful to look at, but to be truly loved, quilts have to be felt. Tell me, if you met someone today, someone who asked you what you do with your quilts, how ever would you put your depth of feeling into words?

I COME WITH ATTACHMENTS

WHEN I WAS IN FOURTH GRADE, MY TEACHER HAD A row of books lined up on a shelf in the back of the room. If we paid attention to our grammar work sheet and finished it quickly, we were allowed to go back and choose a book to read until the rest of the class was done. One day I found a book on that shelf that I loved and have carried in my head the rest of my life. It had two charming creatures in it named Nip and Tuck. They lived on an island. One had a fish hook that grew on the end of his tail, and he sat on the end of the dock and caught his dinner every day. The other had a spoon and fork for hands. He was a salad eater. What a convenient life! Their tools were always at hand (pun intended).

I have quilter friends whose tools are always nearby, if not at hand. They are neat people. Some of these friends have pegboards, and each pair of scissors—each spool of thread—has its own place. Their houses are clean. There are no needles in the carpet. Their stencils are filed on pegs by category and size. There are never any threads on their floors or on their furniture and clothes, either. The threads, of course, are in the waste-basket. Their quilts are folded and refolded and stored with no stress or creases.

My friends' ironing boards always look like new. The covers on them are crisp and shiny, and usually they have something clever on them, like pictures of bouquets or lines and charts to lay out quilt blocks and bias strips perfectly. Their irons, of course, are shiny. Sitting beside them are full bottles of distilled water. In their closets there are bins or boxes or little crates that hold fabrics, which are not only divided into color categories, but are folded nicely and layered into color gradations.

There is a commodious wastebasket that is empty except for the clean plastic bag liner. And they all have a desk! Oh, yes, a desk! It has a lamp and a secretary's chair, the kind that you adjust to your posture. It is adjusted, of course. The desk has drawers filled with neat supplies like buttons and pins and coiled tape measures. Next to the desk is the sewing machine in a polished cabinet (the most elegant one the store sells). The machine has two options. It can be neatly folded into the cabinet, and then the exposed wood is polished with lemon oil, or the machine will be raised into the "ready" position. It will be covered with a sewing machine cover that my friend has made herself. It is made of striped ticking and has a perfectly machine-appliqued miniature sewing machine decorating it.

In all honesty to my friends, I see their sewing rooms when I am invited to have "lunch with the quilters," or when I am visiting from a distant place, and they generously put me up for the night. When I gasp at their amazing organization and cleanliness, they always smile secretly. Let me say this right here and now: "I don't believe you."

– – – –

Like my storybook creatures, we are born with God-given tools fastened to our bodies. Because they are attached, we know where they are when we need them, and we don't need to find a place to store them. For instance, we have fingers. We use them for cutting, holding, and stitching. I, myself, use my right thumbnail for pushing my quilting needle, which is why my nail has three holes in it. We have hands that we use for opening doors and holding irons. We use our legs to carry us to the quilt store. If I am spreading out my quilt lining and batting to baste them together, I use my feet (one on each of two corners) and my hands (on each of the other two corners) to stretch and hold them in place. Then, I insert big pins into the rug to hold the corner down, and my hands and feet are then free for other chores.

The best attached tool we have is our head. Aside from having a mouth, which is a great food receptacle, it works fine for thinking. It plays with shapes and colors and puts them all together for a quilt. My head also has ears on it, to hold up my glasses.

Though we have basic tools attached, our lives are certainly enriched by the tools that we may consider accessories—my glasses, for instance. It took some training to remember that when I take off my glasses to squint at print fabric in order to determine its color and value, I must remember to hang them by one of the ear pieces from the neckline of my dress. For some years I made a trip at least once a month to the optometrist to have a

– – – –

lens reinserted after I had put them down, forgotten them, and sat on them. I have finally schooled myself in the art of dangling my glasses most of the time. There are none more foolish than nearsighted friends who lose their glasses when they have pushed them up onto the tops of their heads.

We have places for our "attachments" but if we are honest, we must admit that we rarely, if ever, put them there. For instance, a needle belongs in a needle, case on a shelf. My needles are not in a case. If I drop a needle and I am at home, I make a brief hunt. I warn my family, especially my husband, who likes to walk around in his socks. Then, when I am all through with my quilting, I get down and run a magnet around the floor. In the end, I run my vacuum, which always finds the needle and drives it either into the rug or bends it. Today I found one protruding straight ahead through the rubber bumper of the vacuum, looking like some fiendish assault weapon from the thirteenth century.

Storing spools of thread neatly is a challenge, mostly because they unwind, roll, and come in various sizes. I try to keep them in their places by filing them in jelly roll pans. I am sure they would be neater if I could discipline myself to slip the thread ends into the notches on the spools—if I could find the notches. What's more, I have a lot of spools of thread and a lot of jelly roll pans, which I stack. Because of the various sizes of the spools, they are uneven and, from time to time, the entire pile

– – – –

of pans shifts and slips and dumps. This is a good time to regroup, resort, rewind, and rearrange.

Some of us have boxes of sewing machine attachments, an assortment of rulers, all kinds of markers, patterns, and so on. The biggest challenge of all is to fold and file our fabrics. When we make a quilt, we can go to the store and buy the fabric we need and cut it up. But if we save and stash, if we have snippets and shreds, strips and selvedges, neat storage becomes an impossible dream.

I have begun to deal with some of my rubble. I am throwing away the old pulp-paper patterns that I collected 20 to 30 years ago. The extra space will give me half a shelf in my floor-to-ceiling bookcase. Maybe then I can get some of the books picked up that are piled on the floor.

I have spent some time today trying to get my world in order. I have put a door on legs to make a long, slender table, and I have placed it beneath a row of windows in my workroom. On it, I have put my markers, my threads, my glue—the bits and pieces of my days. On the couch I have lined up boxes, each one holding a project and its parts. I have scooped up my sewing-machine enhancements and piled them on my unpolished and well-used cabinet. I know, in general, where these things are now. They are arranged in order, but these are working tools. I use them—the stubby pencils, the prickly pincushions. There will always be threads on my floor and

- - - -

pins under my chairs, but without the slag heap I have always had, perhaps it will be easier to find the gold.

I find that, aside from my basic attached equipment, I have an astonishing array of options. It would be nice if life were neat and compartmentalized like the lives of Nip and Tuck, those two make-believe creatures from my childhood, the ones with all of their attachments in place. Our lives are more complicated than theirs, but we could simplify by making a stab at straightening out our quilting confusion.

Once upon a time, this quilter worked very hard and sorted and arranged, and she got herself totally organized and absolutely neat. Do you believe in fairy tales?

MIXED BLESSINGS

WEDNESDAY IS MINE. IT IS THE HIGH POINT OF MY WEEK. It's the day I meet with an amazing group of women, quilters who range in age from somewhere in their thirties to their mid-eighties. Sometimes as few as four are present. Sometimes there are as many as 12 or 13.

Each Wednesday, we gather to tie quilts for hospices and shelters. Just like other groups that gather together across the country, these women meet to give their precious time and energy as their personal gifts. Not all are quilters, but they all join in and find talents that they had not dreamed of.

We gather in a room where the sun floods in across a rose garden. In winter, mounds of snow bank against the windows. Each person has chosen how to spend her time. Several work on the floor, spreading out patchwork blocks, arranging them into quilt tops. Some sit around a table with an unfinished comforter spread out in front of them. They poke giant needles through the quilt layers and tie colorful yarn knots. One young woman brings her sewing machine and churns out sturdy denim quilts for men and boys. Another sets up her machine and sews on the first stitches of the bindings, and then I take over, folding those binding strips up over the raw, exposed edges of the quilts and stitching them down, the finishing touch. I do this because it is a mindless job. It requires no special abilities and no

- - - -

forethought, and it leaves me free to enjoy being with these women as I sew, over and over, around and around.

My friends are bright, funny, and caring, like the women I've met in similar groups in town halls, churches, and museums. As much alike as they are, they are a diverse group. They all come for a variety of reasons: some because they feel the need to be part of this generous experience, and some originally came out of curiosity. Some of the women come for a time of relief, to be away from the pressures and demands of their professional lives. Others are retirees who spend other days driving for Meals on Wheels or tutoring school children. One woman brings Hobey each week, her teddy bear–like yellow lab, in training to be a Helping Paws dog. He lies beneath a table pretending to be asleep, but one eye is always partially open, watching. Each of these generous, busy women comes ostensibly to make quilts, but in all honesty, they come for the pleasure of being together.

At noon we stack our finished work in cupboards and go out to the corner restaurant for soup and salads. We sit around a table in perfect order, the left-handed quilters on the right, and the right-handed quilters on the left, and Hobey in the middle. We laugh a lot, and I feel privileged to be counted among them.

What is the mystery about quilting? How does it bring out such amiability, such charity in people? If you were

– – – –

to try to categorize these friends of mine and sort them into groups of interests or talents or backgrounds, you would find the job amazingly difficult. Yet these people fit together so snugly. The wonder is that such a con-glomeration of human beings can form such a close, perfect circle, all because of needles and thread.

TOUCH-ME-NOT

THERE WAS A LADY IN THE RESTAURANT ON FRIDAY NIGHT. I saw her as she worked her way across the room and stood beside our table. She was wearing leopard-spotted stretch pants. Because she was young and slender, those pants simply clung and flowed and glowed around her body like a proper quilt. I wanted to reach out and touch her. I did not. The laws of acceptable behavior say quite definitely that one does not feel a lady's leopard-print pants in a restaurant.

Right up there at the top of the list of those rules of acceptable behavior about feeling things is this one, "Thou shalt not touch a quilt." At least, not without permission. I say this knowing that you and I, as quilters, are tactile people. We ache to touch, and to feel, and to caress quilts. Of all of the senses with which we are blessed, touch is perhaps the one with which we are most obsessed. Which do you suppose came first, the love of feeling fabric, or the delight of putting little pieces together to create whole cloth?

The need to feel things is a part of all our days. Watch those about you reaching out to fondle the surfaces and textures around them. I can trace my own love back to the time when, as a tiny child, I used to traipse after my mother through stores. Her admonition was always, "Remember, do not touch," and I would ball up my fists and stuff my hands into my pockets so that I would not be

– – – –

45

tempted to feel the little metal points of the tinny toy cars, the miraculous, tiny, loopy stitches on the edges of lace handkerchiefs, and the coarse feel of the lavender seeds in sachets. Today, as I stand at the tables in quilt shops, chatting and waiting for my two yards of fabric to be cut, I watch the sales clerks fingering my bolts of loveliness, stroking the fabric subconsciously. It makes my fingers twitch.

Even though, with our other senses, we see things, taste food, smell aromas, and hear gentle music, I wonder if feeling is not the most basic of our pleasures. Our very vocabulary expresses this instinct. When we are emotional, we speak of our hearts being "touched." We say that we have a touch of rheumatism, or an artist's touch at the piano. We speak with a touch of sarcasm, a generous person is a soft-touch, and an airplane touches down. Perhaps my favorite word is touchstone, which is the symbol of quality, that thing by which we measure all other things, a sign of goodness.

I am a quilter, and I love fabric. I love that glassy feeling of satin, that soft, mysterious feel of velvet. I love that honest roughness of gritty burlap and that warm gentleness of my cottons when I take them fresh and sweet from the dryer. I am a quilter.

I love, too, the precise feel of flat seams and accurate joinings. I love the glowy feeling of the aura of light as it reflects from the swirls and feathers and flowers on my quilts. I just plain love the feel of a quilt and the deep joy

- - - -

of touching it. Quilters love to touch. Even though the official, white-gloved ladies at quilt shows are most obliging and will turn back the corners of the displays for you to see the bindings and stitching and labels, when their backs are turned, bewitched fingers reach out to touch those quilts. We need to remind ourselves that because this need to feel things is such an integral part of our beings, we should ball up our fists and thrust them into our pockets.

There is a lovely little wildflower that grows beside streams, leaning out across rocks, its delicate leaves and brilliant blossoms flirting with the playing waters below. The tiny flowers are scarlet and orange and yellow and they are sometimes called jewelweed. Dangling from the rambling stems of these flowers are small green pods. If you touch the tips of these pods, they burst, flinging their seeds down into the rocky pool below. This plant's other name is touch-me-not.

This fragile plant is a miracle. It is perfection in its wild and natural state, and knowing the astonishing surprise that happens when exploring fingers touch them and the pods explode, will help us to remember the threat in our own honest, exploring fingers. Quilters are a touchy-feely kind of people. We feel happy, we feel blue, and we feel excited about quilts. And above all, we feel strongly about treasuring our quilts and keeping them clean and strong and perfect. Those little gem-colored flowers remind us: TOUCH-ME-NOT!

– – – –

SWEET MYSTERY

WHEN THE WEATHER TURNS COLD IN THIS PART OF THE country, when the first snow flakes drift down in the winter sky, people rush out into the cold with eyes glowing and mufflers flying. Bare ears turn red and wind ruffles the hair on uncovered heads. Steps quicken and people move along filled with the very goodness of life. Those who live here love the chill of the first snowfall— and the next—and the next. Some people were born to thrive in ice and snow.

Apparently it's turnabout with people who come from the southern parts of this country. My Kansas daughter has been visiting. Right now, here in the Northland, we are in the midst of a heat wave. Six months ago we thought we would never be warm again. Now, we swelter. My daughter stopped in at the dry cleaners this morning. The pleasant proprietor had perspiration spilling down his forehead. His shirt was glued to his shoulder blades.

"Well," he said to her, "is it hot enough for you?"

"Not really!" she replied.

My daughter has lived away from here long enough that her body chemistry has gone through an evolution. It has adapted southward. Through her veins now flows a different blood. She is comfortable with heat. She goes about her daily activities undaunted by weather that would put me flat on my back in front of a blasting fan

– – – –

or submerged to my shoulders in a grandchild's inflatable pool in the backyard. Were I to live in Kansas in the summer, I would be a helpless blob. I have never honestly thought of myself as a northerner, but I can understand why people here make quilts, why people sleep under warm quilts, wear warm quilted clothing, and hang quilts across frosted windows.

So, why do people make quilts in the South? Could it be that quilts are something more than warmth? Are they something beyond practical? Of course, you and I have always known that they are. We know that if we want shelter and protection, we can buy a blanket, turn up the furnace, or put on the storm windows. If they weren't something more than useful, why else would all of us quilt through perspiration and sticky hands when the thought of keeping warm is the last thing on our minds? Aye, there's the mystery of it!

As quilters we have been beseiged by inquiring researchers. There have been questionnaires from university sociology departments, theses from graduate students, and editorial interviews. They all ask the same questions: Why is quilting so alluring? What is this unquenchable appetite we have that separates us from the fainthearted craft dabblers? What is the vision we see?

Fashion designers portray the desirable woman as one in a filmy dress, her mysteries hidden. Movies feature the temptress as a solitary lady, standing in a corner,

– – – –

veiled. There is nothing exciting in revelation, in flesh and bones, in identification.

I propose that perhaps the mystery is an aspect of quilting that should be cherished, not exposed, not explained. Quilting is seductive, exciting. It lures us from the things we should be doing. It flirts with us. It is intriguing. I love a mystery.

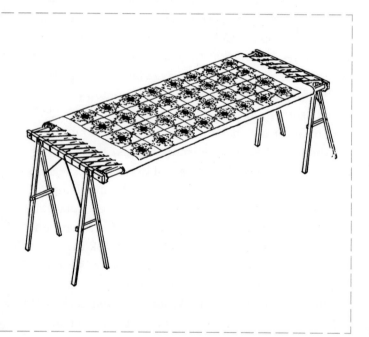

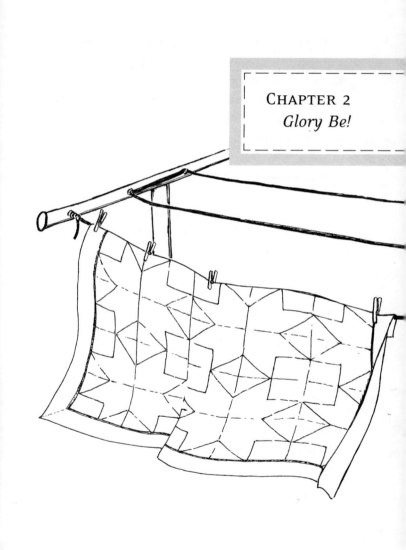

CHAPTER 2
Glory Be!

ON NECESSITY AND INVENTION

I HAVE A THEORY THAT THE DIFFERENCE BETWEEN A really good quilt and an acceptable quilt is that a good quilter knows how to "fix it." Every quilter faces at least one crisis with each quilt. Sometimes these crises are horrific enough to send lesser people into deep depressions, perhaps abandon the project altogether. Some quilters tackle the repair job with creativity, producing surprises even they had not expected.

Since every one of us is faced with these dilemmas and must make decisions as to whether or not to invest energy in coping, the choices made are what separate the women from the girls, the men from the boys, and bring to the fore the real geniuses.

Enough said! I've listed some of the most common crises here. How would you triumph over these disasters? Test yourself with this Quilt-Coper Quiz: What would you do...

1. When you cut out 5,280 pieces and only afterwards discover that the fabric has a definite up-and-down print?

2. When you realize that you have cut your four border strips each 1" short?

3. When you lay out your finished top on the kitchen table and discover that you have a grease spot in the center of the medallion?

– – – –

4. When you draw a penciled quilting line 1" off the mark and haven't a prayer to cover it?

5. When you sit down to quilt your all-white quilt and realize that there is a 12" long black thread trapped between the batt and the top?

6. When you drop your scissors point-down into the quilt as it is stretched in the frame.

7. When the cat scampers in from the rain and leaves a diagonal trail of muddy paw marks across your framed quilt?

8. When you discover that you have left a large-headed pin inside your finished quilt?

9. When you hang up your quilted wall hanging and, instead of hanging smoothly, it ripples like waves lapping on the beach?

There! Did you cope? Did you cure these problems? Whatever your solutions to these quilt catastrophes have been, the finished quilt will bear your own unique imprint.

Moral: Don't abandon hope, all ye who blunder here! Remember, perseverance is the mother of invention.

– – – –

FITTING AND PROPER

AS I WAS CHANGING SHEETS ON THE BEDS THIS MORNING, I studied my daughter's queen-sized waterbed in the basement bedroom. Spread across it is the first quilt she ever made. It was meant to be a present for Bill and me, to cover our own bed, with a dust ruffle skirting below it. It is a stunning quilt of blue and white diamonds. But as it happens, it fits Connie's bed perfectly, and that is where it has stayed. It measures 75 inches across, and if she had meant it for that bed originally, it couldn't have been calculated more exactly.

Fit is important. I recently went out to buy a dress to wear for my granddaughter's wedding. In the fitting room, I struggled into a variety of dresses of chiffon and linen and other exotic fibers. Nothing went over my lumpy body properly until I found a very, very expensive, mandarin-style silk dress in a glossy green-blue color. That one slid over my head and shoulders and hips like a glove. It was worth every cent I paid for it.

Now, here's the catch: It never occurred to me, when I was in the fitting room, to try sitting down in that dress. On the day of the wedding, after I got ready, I tried to get into the car to drive to the ceremony. I found that I couldn't lift my knee to put my foot inside. The dress hobbled me like a mummy wrap. I shimmied the skirt

- - - -

56

up a bit to release my knees, and then eased my body into the seat to sit in a semi-reclining position. In a sitting position, the dress bound me tightly across the hips. It was obviously not a good fit.

I am a quiltmaker. I stopped sewing dresses long ago when store-bought dresses became less expensive than those I could make at home. I felt I would rather invest in fabric to make quilts instead. I also realized that quilts do not have to be darted, shaped, and hemmed. In other words, fitted. When I make quilts, I can work with straight edges, standard sizes, and flat surfaces. Working in prescribed basic elements takes the guesswork out of the simple things. It leaves me free to be imaginative, dramatic, or whimsical with the important parts, the color and the design. When I make a quilt, I don't have to make alterations to make it fit. I don't have to tweak and tuck. I don't have to interface collars and sew buttonholes. I don't have to pin my way around a movable hem. Quilts don't need all that rigamarole.

Looking down at Connie's bed with its perfectly fitted quilt, I realize how important quilt fit is, but it's an easier kind of fit. A properly fitting quilt fills that space on the wall, or covers the great long frame of a gangly, high school basketball star, or tucks into a tiny baby's bassinet, but there are forgiving variables. It just takes

– – – –

an inch here and there to get flat, even sides and surfaces. That's what makes fitting quilts tolerable.

I have devised an exercise program to make my body slim and trim. I want that green-blue silk Mandarin dress to fit me, and I've decided I would rather rearrange my body than alter that dress. I'll use my sewing know-how and my golden hours, instead, to make my quilts.

This, my friend, you might say, is a fitting tribute.

– – – –

THE NAME'S THE GAME

ON A BIBLE QUILT I MADE, THERE IS A BLOCK WITH A cheerful children's picture of Adam naming the animals in the Garden of Eden. A ship naming is celebrated by breaking a bottle of champagne across the bow of the vessel. Ribbon-cutting ceremonies and toasts accompany the namings of tall buildings and corporate mergers. Christening a child is a more solemn occasion. Naming things is important.

Driving on our county road recently, I passed the Twin Lakes Clinic, not far from a community called Hilltop with a tree-lined Elm Street threading through the center of town. New housing developments are springing up with romantic titles like Winter Bluff or Cedar Creek. The names identify the character of places.

So it is with quilt blocks. Many of their names described the surroundings of the eighteenth-century quiltmakers. Those blocks were called Log Cabin, Tall Pine Tree, Corn and Beans, or The Rocky Road to Kansas, and there is certainly no hole in my barn door, and yet I make these blocks because they are my link to all of those quiltmakers before me.

Now, we are seeing funny, relevant new names, which are modern-day salutes to the endurance of the tradition and the whimsy of quiltmaking. Many new quilts may resemble those of past times, but look closely at them. The names of these quilts give us clues to their

– – – –

novelty. Today, if you look closely at a Hawaiian quilt, what appears to be cut-out, appliqued tropical flowers, may, instead, be personal symbols. Baltimore-style quilts have been cropping up at quilt shows with designs created from the carefully cut motifs of landmarks to be found far from Chesapeake Bay. Sunbonnet Sue has jogged across contemporary America, handled managerial positions in the corporate structure, and produced stunning art works on these new quilts. Our traditions have been redone in interesting, fresh ways, some so subtle and clever that we might well miss their intent if it were not for the naming clues.

These upbeat names indicate that today's quilters lead diverse lives. Today's quilts may display a bucolic view of farm life, or they may embody a modern art concept, or reflect an intercontinental travel experience. They may be carefully hand drafted, or may be skillfully spun from a computer in sophisticated angles and colors. Today's quilters have worldwide resources and can use an array of salvaged scraps of dress materials, batiks, kimono silks, or marbleized home-dyed muslins. At once universal and personal, naming these quilts gives them a meaningful place in our time. Naming them is to bless them.

In other words, quilts are as much a part of the quiltmaker as a child, or a home, or a moment of joy. Wander through your next quilt show and read these

– – – –

new names. Imagine the moment that the vision of this quilt was conceived, the pleasure of the piecing and putzing, and the sense of accomplishment when the quilt was finally bound off and the last thread cut. Then, imagine the moment of naming it, and know that a quilt by any other name would never be as sweet.

IT'S ALWAYS AN ADVENTURE

WE WENT ON A TRIP LAST WEEKEND TO GET AWAY FROM city pressures. Bill and I left behind the mailman and the telephone and the computer and all of the small requests for our time and money that we deal with every day. We drove far enough away along country roads to feel that we were having a holiday, just the two of us. The wildflowers were breathtaking. Whole fields of Queen Anne's lace looked as if it had snowed. Cornflowers along the edges of the road bordered our path with heavenly blue. There were fields of purple asters and rich yellow butter-and-eggs. The area below our hotel room had been designated as a Prairie Preserve, and it was so filled with black-eyed Susans that it looked as if molten gold had been poured across the hillside.

On Saturday afternoon, we left the car on the street beside the softball field in the town park, and we went walking. When thunder began to growl and lightning twittered in the distance, we hurried back to our car, only to find it filled with shattered glass from the windshield. Some ball player had hit a powerful line drive right through the glass. The lightning became alarming, and we hurriedly picked shards from the seats before scrambling inside for shelter.

While Bill mopped the dashboard and wheel with pieces of wet paper towel to pick up some of the splintery bits, a tornado warning siren sounded almost simultaneously

– – – –

with the pelting of hail as the storm hit us furiously. We huddled inside as the storm rocked and buffeted us.

The next day, Bill covered the jagged wound in the windshield with plastic tape, and driving at a prudent speed, we headed home past battered fields, along a path of broken tree branches. We felt quite triumphant, though. We had coped.

Life is like that! We go from one crisis to the next, grappling and problem-solving. Making a quilt is like that, too. Some quiltmakers are calm and controlled. They seem to make wonderful quilts easily and perfectly, but I don't believe for a moment that these quiltmakers do it without crises. That's the fun of quiltmaking—dealing, from moment to moment, with the challenges. Think of the uncertainty that we have when we unfold three yards of spanking new, untouched fabric. How do you want to cut into it? That first snip takes courage. Think of the feeling of laying out a finished quilt top made of 5,280 pieces carefully stitched together, only to discover that the undisciplined mass of material has come to life, all lumpy and rumply. How will you find a way to tame it to lie flat and and trim so that you can quilt it? Think of the challenge of finding that you have used up all of one fabric and must substitute, replace, reshape, or salvage something else to finish your quilt.

Apparently this struggle is a common theme among humans; just watch old Laurel and Hardy movies. My

– – – –

favorite line in them has always been when big, pushy Oliver Hardy says to timid Stan Laurel, "Here's another fine mess you've gotten us into!" Well, quiltmaking is like that...one fine mess after another, and besting that mess is always an adventure.

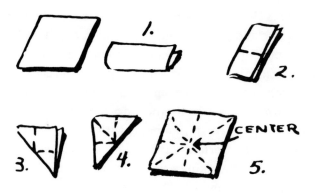

ANOTHER SLANT

BY BEDTIME LAST NIGHT, I HAD MY QUILT HALF BASTED.
Today I'll have this step finished, and I can put the quilt
in my frame. For two or three weeks, I'll be able to stitch
quietly, listening to music, as I watch the patterns swell
and bloom on the surface of my work. Basting a quilt is
perhaps my least favorite thing about quiltmaking, but
it is necessary, like cleaning the vegetables before I can
cook a feast.

I will spend a day or two waddling around on my knees,
wearing out the fabric of my jeans, as I pin, measure,
straighten, and stitch with a giant needle until, finally, I
can lift all three layers and plop them into my frame as
a single unit, ready to go.

I've watched friends prepare quilts by other methods such as pinning the three layers together in a large
frame with small safety pins; or attaching one edge of
the top, batting, and backing to the roller bar of a frame,
and then, quilting from the edge of the quilt, rolling it
round and round as they progress. Some don't baste at
all. They simply stretch the backing layer onto an enormous frame, tack it to the rails of the frame, pat on the
batting, and stretch the top in place, securing it around
the edges with more thumb tacks. They quilt from the
edges and roll it to the center. It seems to work for them.
Not me!

– – – –

When I began making quilts, I tried all these ways, and I got some pretty unusual results. Now, with my work stretched out, pinned to the carpet, and carefully basted, my quilts are generally flat, straight-seamed, and square-cornered when they are finished.

Years ago, Bill took me to the Math Trauma Clinic. I can do math reasonably well, but the emotional stress of calculating numbers fills me with anxiety. At the clinic, I learned two important things: my methods for solving problems do not fit into any norm; and it's not important how a person does a thing as long as the person gets the right results. Now I have the freedom to do the things I do in the way that I do them best. I am now confident to go about my problem-solving challenges in my own way. Sometimes the way that works for me may be "the hard way." Basting quilts on my knees, inching my way around and around on the floor for hours, is not easy, but it works for me.

Sometimes my quilting friends will ask me if they are "allowed" to do things in unconventional ways. They might ask, for instance, if they can applique down the stubborn edge of a unit that is giving them trouble or whether they can use both hand and machine quilting on the same quilt. The only criterion for making a quilt, I tell them, should be personal. The simple guideline should be: "Does this work for ME?" Books and classes give us a starting point and teach us basic skills, but making a quilt shouldn't be about rules; it should be

- - - -

about knowing ourselves and what is most comfortable for our hands. Each of us has to decide what pleases us most, and what will best help our own vision take shape and blossom. Let's be creative and use our individual talents. When we make quilts, whatever we do is okay. What is important is that the process is satisfying and the quilt gives us pleasure.

SIREN SONG

FORTUNATELY, MY SEWING MACHINE HAS BROKEN DOWN. The reciprocal motion of the feed dogs that inches the fabric along beneath the presser foot suddenly will not reciprocate. When I try to stitch, the fabric simply lies there under the foot, accumulating stitches in a great big lump. I have tried all the tricks: turning the machine off, then on again, to try and readjust the computer; dropping the feed dogs and raising them again; and finally dragging the fabric through with brute force in the hopes that the machine will understand that I mean business and that it will behave. Nothing works.

The reason that I say "fortunately" is because I shouldn't be sewing in the first place. I have other things that I need to do. I have a quilt in the frame that needs to be finished, and my bags need to be packed for a quilt conference. Yesterday, however, I got a wonderful package of fabric in the mail. I have been enchanted with the idea of piecing a San Francisco quilt, and a friend has been painting some fabric for me to look like misty Bay Area fog. When I tore open the wrapping and examined the material, I pushed my quilting frame aside and stepped over my suitcases. I got out the pieced San Francisco houses that I had waiting for this new quilt. I played with them, laying them across my misty fabric. I was so excited, in fact, that I whipped out my handy rotary cutter, threaded my sewing machine, and threw myself totally into this new project.

- - - -

By bedtime, I had worked myself into a dithery state and tossed and turned all night with ideas roiling around in my head. The other quilt languished in its frame, and my empty suitcases lay open on the floor. Obviously, I have no self-discipline at all.

This morning my life and my workroom are still in a mess. Sadly, when my sewing machine suddenly ceased its perfect, even stitching, I was flooded with the heavy-hearted knowledge that I must be a responsible person. I should put away my playthings and get on with the chores that need to be done. Sometimes a woman's gotta do what a woman's gotta do.

A new quilt is like the Lorelei to me, like the rock in the Rhine River where the Siren sat, luring the sailors, calling them to wreck their ships upon the reef. In the same way, this new quilt has beckoned to me. It has sung a mysterious, compelling song. It has enticed me and and my resolve is nearly wrecked upon the rock. All of the debris, the dangling threads, and the fabric snippets that surround me are engulfing. I find the prospect of this new quilt enchanting and I cannot save myself.

So now you understand why I say, "Fortunately, my sewing machine has broken." If it had not, I would be surrounded by this new project with the waves of my unfinished things swamping me. After I deliver my sewing machine to the repair man, I will come home and pack my bag for my quilt conference. Then, I will sit

– – – –

down in this lovely sunshine that is spilling through my workroom window, and I will finish that other quilt, the one still in the frame. I will be smart, I will be organized, and I will be obedient, but not by choice.

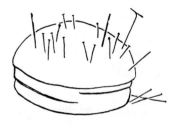

HIND SIGHT

I'M MAKING AN OCEAN WAVES WALL HANGING. WELL, as a matter of fact, I am making several Ocean Waves wall hangings; six, to be exact. Right now, I am immersed in my Japanese Waves. Let's see, where do I start this story? At the beginning, I guess. Let's go back to last November.

One of my daughters decided she wanted to make an Ocean Waves quilt—a king-size one—in three weeks so that she could get it in the mail for Christmas. I dropped everything I had planned to do, including meal making, laundry, and shopping, all the things I would rather not spend time on. Because this huge quilt was to be a scrap quilt, I begged pieces of fabric from every quilter I knew, and then I got out my rotary cutter and board. I washed, pressed, and cut triangles while my daughter, Connie, sat at the machine and stitched them together. The top was done in two weeks, and because of the pressure of time, we tied the quilt in another week, bound it off, and got it in the mail.

Then I got to looking at that ordinary, very usual, predictable Ocean Waves pattern and things started sloshing in my head. I began to see all sorts of great things rising and falling in those triangles. I caught sea fever, and I set sail upon my Waves. In the next five weeks I made a quilt top a week; six tops in all. That's a lot of quilt tops. I bought a gigantic piece of wide backing

- - - -

and a huge batt and spread the tops out on the floor, sandwiching them one at a time. The first four went into the frame, one after another, and I quilted each differently but fairly traditionally. The simple challenge each time was what to do with the borders, the five big central squares, and the large border triangles.

Those first four are finished. This morning I laid out the next top, the one that was inspired by a Japanese woodcut picture. Of all these waves, this is the design that fell short. My Monet top has water lilies floating on the waves, exactly as a "Monet" should, but this "Japanese Woodcut" has turned out to have a personality all its own. It is dominated by the strong geometrics. I have lost my huge wave and my mountain and the swamped fishing boat. The design is rather interesting, but it is definitely different from the antique Japanese picture that inspired it. I made this quilt top because I liked the woodcut and because I wanted to have a "Japanese Woodcut" wall hanging. What to do?

This morning I stood and stared at that quilt top laid out on the floor and wondered if I could reclaim it, make it do what I had originally planned, rather than settle for a rather interesting quilt that is totally unrelated to the original inspiration.

Some years ago, a dear English quilter friend wrote to me to tell me that someone had sent her an American quilt top to finish. From her description I knew she must have a pieced Grandmother's Flower Garden. Because

– – – –

she was a North Country quilter, whose forte is whole-cloth quilting, she gazed at that Grandmother's Flower Garden top for days, and suddenly it spoke to her, and she knew what to do with it. She put it into a frame upside down, and quilted it from the back. That way, she said, the American lady would have an American quilt on the front, and an English quilt on the back.

The story came flooding back to me and told me what to do with my Japanese Ocean Waves. It told me to mark the back of the quilt with a drawing of the original picture of the woodcut. I have put the quilt into the frame upside down, and I am quilting the Japanese waves into it. I love what is happening, and I haven't even turned it over to see what it looks like on the pieced side. I hope that the quilting design traces all the shading from the original woodcut that I worked into the piecing on the front. My quilting stitches may not even show among the storm of triangles on the front. They may simply serve as an anchor to hold the quilt layers together, but the back is a different story, and what's happening under my quilting needle is exciting.

When I am done, I will have a two-sided quilt. I can admire the pieced triangles that dart across the front, or, like my English friend, I can turn it over and enjoy the quilted picture on the back side. The tumult of that Japanese ocean storm is going to add dimension and a new depth to my waves.

– – – –

THANKS, I NEEDED THAT!

SOMETIMES I FEEL LIKE NO ONE UNDERSTANDS. I FEEL like I am a person alone in my world. And then I remember that I am a quilter and that there are thousands of you out there in my world and that you all understand. Sometimes, I need to talk. May I talk to you?

I'm making a quilt that needs to look as if it had chocolate sauce spilled on it. I've looked everywhere for just the right chocolate-sauce material. I've fingered polished cottons and felts and suedes and satins. I've covered all the fabric shops in town, pulling up in front in my rusty station wagon and trotting in. I've pulled bolts from the shelves, squinting at them in the natural light and under the glare of fluorescence. I've folded them. I've scrunched them.

The other day, I stopped in at a fabric shop in an affluent part of town. The other customers were stockinged and mascaraed. Their expensive sweaters were coordinated with their lovely tweedy skirts. I was, by contrast, arrayed in my usual pink jogging suit with dirty knees and an overlay of snippets and threads. My shoes were scruffy, my face undecorated, my nails unmanicured. I was, after all, in the midst of making my quilt, and I was dressed for it. If I had had a shopping cart in tow, I might very well have been mistaken for a bag lady.

– – – –

As I walked into that store, I spotted a bolt of fabric high on a shelf that looked as if it had chocolate sauce oozing all over. The light played across it, bringing out the highlights of the velveteen. It was deep and soft. It was delicious.

The price tag said $12.95. "Wow," I said. "That's expensive chocolate sauce."

The clerk was a young girl. She, too, was dressed meticulously. She was not dressed for working on a quilt. "Let's see, I wonder how many inches I will need of this." I said. The velveteen felt soft in my hand. I was itching to stitch it.

Out came a scrap of paper from my pocket. Out came a pencil. "I'll take two-thirds yard of this." I said.

"We only cut in eighth's." She didn't smile. She looked down her nose. Obviously, she wished I wasn't in her shop.

"Then," I said. "give me five-eighths of a yard."

It seemed like a weirder way to measure fabric than in quarters or thirds, but she obviously would brook no arguments.

Silently she cut my chocolate-sauce fabric. Silently she folded it and put it in the bag. Silently she accepted my money and punched the cash register. The lady had no sense of humor. She did not understand a fabric-feeling, penny-pinching, thready quilter.

– – – –

That night my phone rang. A friend was calling with a question. "Just a minute," I said. "I have to put down my molasses."

"What in heaven's name are you doing with molasses?" she asked.

"I'm making a chocolate-sauce quilt," I explained. "I've dripped molasses over the top of an inverted cup so that I can watch it drip down the sides. I want to see what a gooey drip looks like. I want to see if it runs down the side in a straight stream or if it wanders. I want to see if the pool in the saucer globs up or runs smoothly in an even circle away from the drip. What was it you wanted?"

"Oh!" said my friend. "Never mind, dear. You go back to your molasses." She was not a quilter. She didn't understand that I was getting ready to stitch chocolate sauce and that I needed to see how sauce behaves. My molasses experiment sounded like pre-school messing to her.

My neighbor just dropped in to borrow an egg. I heard her knock on the back door, and I called out for her to come in because I was lying on my back under my quilt frame, looking up at the plain white back of my chocolate quilt. I was studying whether it was quilted evenly and adequately. You and I know that it's easier to judge the value of quilting when your eye isn't confused by all the color and riot of lines on the

– – – –

top. There I lay, flat on my back, staring up. "Help your-self," I said, "the eggs are in the refrigerator."

My neighbor is a lovely lady. We have been friends for twenty-five years. For twenty-five years she has thought I was a little eccentric but harmless.

I suppose there are things that you and I do that the rest of the world simply does not understand. It moves along in its pleasantly groomed, well-behaved manner. I will admit that I do not approach life as most of my neighbors do. Do you? Don't we get caught up in the enthusiasm of our quilting? Don't we approach our work with unique eyes? We are, after all, doing creative work. We are creative people.

I am a creative person. I make quilts! Quilts are a good thing to make. I am a good person. There, I've said it. Thanks so much. I just needed to talk.

– – – –

SECURITY BLANKET

ONCE AGAIN, I'VE LOST THE HUBCAP ON THE RIGHT front side of my car. It is lying out there somewhere in the weeds beside the road. Those big metal discs are expensive. With winter here, I have to protect that exposed wheel hub. After this latest loss, I bought a package of cheap heavy-duty, high-impact plastic hubcaps. They look just like the heavy-duty, metal, real thing at a fraction of the price. Now, when I lose a hubcap again, I will not weep.

When I brought the box of hubcaps home, Bill took out the four shiny platters and laid them in a row. They are classy looking. Arcing slits, cut into the plastic, radiate out from the center. Bill, the engineer, mused over them.

"Do you realize," he said, "that when you put them on your car, the design will spin in opposite directions on the two sides? On one side, they will spin to the front. On the other side, they will spin toward the back." This imbalance disturbed him.

"I don't imagine that anybody can see both sides of my car at the same time. Nobody will notice," I said.

"Somebody will," he said darkly. (Probably another engineer.)

Later that day, I laid out my current quilt-in-progress on the floor and studied it. Something was not right. Was I troubled by the heaviness of color in the lower-left corner? Was the problem the focal point that flowed from the upper right through the center and drifted off

– – – –

without emphasis? Was my quilt visually lopsided? I went to bed that night, restless and uneasy. What was the matter with my quilt? What was the matter with me?

Balance is a funny concept. If the wheels of a car are unbalanced, the car steers strangely, so that, when you step on the brake pedal, the car will swerve. It is out of control. If your bank balance is wrong and out of control, you are in big trouble. What is so comforting about having our lives, our cars, our money, and our quilts in balance?

When I am putting together a new quilt, I often leave it in the middle of the floor of my workroom so that everyone who comes to the door can squint at it and tell me if it "feels" right. I study it through my reducing glass and move things around on it to try to balance it. I am open to the suggestions that everyone offers. Playing with my quilt is part of the fun of its making.

If I can make the symmetry of design flow, it gives the quilt grace. It gentles harsh lines and colors. It gives it balance. Along with the softness of the fabric and the joy of creation, perhaps working with that rhythm and proportion, that balance, is what I find so satisfying in making a quilt. There is a secure feeling when the world and our quilts are in control.

I looked up the word "balance" in the dictionary, and I found a list of words like "graceful" and "fluent." I found a second list of synonyms for "balance" that included words like "monotonous," "mediocre," and "run of the

- - - -

mill." Strange words to discover when we have been considering the satisfaction and pleasure we can achieve from balanced lives and lines. Can it be that too much balance can become dull and rote like marching wooden soldiers? Row after row after row of perfection? Is perfection boring? Does balance have to be perfection?

I once knew a teacher who had her students lay out their repeating blocks for a quilt, and then she had them turn one block, just one, a quarter turn. It was enough to break those monotonous, marching blocks, and something interesting happened. That variation sparked the quilt to life. It's that bit of difference, a flaw, perhaps, or a wavering from endless precision, a gentle varying that adds a bit of humanity to our quilts, and that is what endears them to us.

I have a theory. I believe that the very best quilts are the ones that have had mistakes made in them, and having made the mistake, the quilter has coped creatively with it. She has used imaginative improvisation to cure the flaw. The perfect, balanced picture has been varied slightly, and in the imperfection, it captures our affection.

I suppose this is the genius and the challenge of our quiltmaking: to make our quilts balanced, a picture of symmetry that comforts us but with an added touch of individual sparkle from our hearts. That difference makes a quilt our own, and it is what makes that quilt a true security blanket.

- - - -

ALL THAT'S GOLD DOES NOT GLITTER

SEVERAL WEEKS AGO, MY MOUTH WAS WHOLE AND HEALTHY. Then one evening, as I was cheerfully crunching away on a piece of peanut brittle, my mouth was suddenly in ruin. One tooth had crumbled. It had disintegrated, and left in its place was a jagged, raggedy peak. I went to the dentist.

Two appointments later, after some filing, sanding, poking, and molding, I returned for my reconstruction. I was going to be like new—recapped and rebuilt.

There is a lot of trust between a dentist and a patient. When you consider that we sit in that reclining, padded chair with our mouth open while this other person puts sharp instruments into it, there is nothing to do but to trust.

I opened my mouth. My dentist pushed a cold, hard, metal form over the remnant of my old tooth. He cut and pasted my new tooth. He pressed it into place. "There," he said as he stood back to admire his work. He leaned his head from side to side. He peered. He smiled. His examining light was brilliant in my face. "Here," he said, and he handed me the mirror.

I paled. I gasped. "Doctor," I said, "it's GOLD."

"Of course," he said.

"But, it twinkles. It sparkles. It's horrible." My recap would not be unnoticeable as I had expected. Instead it would be totally obtrusive in all its glistening glory.

"Now, now," said the dentist.

– – – –

He patted my shoulder. He soothed me. He removed the gold cap, making me promise that if another dentist ever, ever looked into my mouth, I would explain that he did "this" because I "made him do it." Then, he patiently, resignedly buffed it to a dull finish.

As I watched him, it occurred to me that I have tried, so many times, to make gold shine. Gold, in terms of quilting, is quite another situation. When I have tried to create "gold" in my quilting, more often than not I have been faced with a final result that was orange or brown or yellow, but not gold. There have been times when I have tried to make a "silver" design and it has turned drab gray. How do you make these precious metal colors shine in your quilts? Inevitably, I embellish: beads, threads, lamé, sequins. I stitch. I rip. I rivet.

I toss fabrics into heaps on my floor and try to find other fabrics that make a complementary glow or bring out the sparkle. I spend hours at the quilt shop pulling bolts off the shelves to see if some quality is hidden there. I drive miles to other shops to find something new, to dig through their fat quarters and leftover bits. Still and all, if even that doesn't work and the precious luster eludes me, I simply tell people I have been experimenting with the creative uses of orange or brown or gray. It's really so hard to make gold sparkle when you want it to.

– – – –

ALL RIGHT, SEW WHAT?

THIS MORNING I RAN OUT OF FABRIC FOR THE QUILT I am working on. All I needed was enough for a couple more little squares and, even though I dug through the scraps in the wastebasket, there was no way I could eke out those pieces from the last little bits. At 9:30 I drove to the fabric store, clutching my sample in my hot little hand. I searched through the array of bolts lining the walls and, lucky me, there was still some of the lovely, sweet, hot raspberry-colored fabric left. True, I only needed a scrap and the minimum cut was a quarter yard. The thought of buying a quarter yard was ridiculous. Who ever bought just a quarter yard of anything? I thought to myself, "I'll take half a yard—no, a yard, in case I need more, and I'll have enough leftover for another time."

I wrote out a check at the cash register while the shop owner slipped my fabric into a pretty, flowered paper bag. I turned to leave. Then I saw "it."

"It" was a bolt of fabric tucked into a display. The end of the material hung gently, draping over the edge of an antique trunk. The fabric waved to me, beckoned to me. The fabric was like a painted lady, rouged here and there, lined and tinted, seductive and compelling. It was like a Siren, calling to an ancient sailor. The fabric waved to me, beckoned to me. It crooned softly. It sang, "Look at me! I am beautiful! I am here! I am waiting! Love me! Caress me! Take me home."

– – – –

Of course I would buy a yard; no, better make it two, no, five. I brought it home to meet the family. Right now my painted lady is sitting on the chair in my back room, making cooing noises. I should be making supper, but the siren song woos me. She draws me into the workroom again and again. "Come! Come!" she is singing. "Let us do something together. Let us make beautiful music."

So, what is my problem? This is it: That lovely fabric is so wonderful, so delicious, I cannot begin to decide what I want to do with it. I have quilt ideas stored up in my brain, but I don't know which one to choose or where to start. And when I do know, how can I bring myself to cut into that flowing, flawless piece of cloth? Sorting through my list of possibilities, I know that none of my old ideas are right for this bewitching fabric. My new project must be planned specially to show it off. Attic Windows? Stars? Sunshine and Shadows? The simpler the pattern, the easier it will be to do something exciting and creative with it, something that will let it wink in and out, flickering and flirting. Oh, this next quilt must be wonderful, and I am frozen in a state of indecision. What to do? What to do?

My seductress will sit on that chair in my workroom for a week, maybe even for a month. The joy of just looking at her, stopping a moment to touch her powdered cheek, is enough for the moment. Then, one day, suddenly, I will know. I will wake up early one morning and

- - - -

come down to admire my fabric, and a new idea will have worked itself out in my head. The idea will be so sudden and so perfect for my quilt that it will surprise me. I will cut my lovely fabric into little pieces and sew it back together again and the little scraps of excitement will sparkle across my quilt and I will love it. Whatever it will be like, it will be mine, alluring and irresistible, to have and to hold, to love and to cherish from that day forward, forever.

– – – –

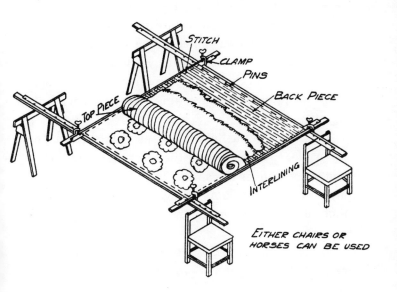

STITCH
CLAMP
PINS
BACK PIECE
TOP PIECE
INTERLINING
EITHER CHAIRS OR
HORSES CAN BE USED

SETTING PRIORITIES

I HAD A RUDE AWAKENING THIS MORNING. ALL NIGHT long, a storm had raged outside. The rain beat against my window, and the wind howled in the chimney. The evergreen tree beneath my bedroom window dug at the side of the house. The whistling and moaning seemed to bury itself deep in its seams.

When I woke, the room was dark. The sun was hidden in the early morning gloom. I had a long list of things to be done today, and so I struggled out of bed. Drowsily, I stepped into the bathroom before heading down the dim stairs. Suddenly, I was jolted awake. Cold water oozed between my toes and lapped at my naked heels. It slithered out beyond the reach of my foot. The bathroom floor was inundated. The ceiling must have been leaking all night.

I switched on the light and inspected the flood. The water gleamed on the cold tile. It encircled the toilet and seeped under the sink. Slimy water dripped into my hair from above. As I moved, the wet hem of my nightie slapped around my ankles. It was not a pleasant situation.

I opened the linen closet and pulled out towels and mopped. I pulled out more towels and sopped up more water and wrung out the towels and I sopped some more. I took the time to run down the stairs to turn on the coffeemaker. Coffee would lift my spirits.

- - - -

The rain beat. The wind moaned. The tree scratched and thumped steadily, sounding much like a grave-digger at work. I mopped, and I dried.

Now, it is sometime later. I have had my coffee and a hot, warming shower. I have put on dry, comforting clothes. The radio is playing rollicking music. Somehow, I find that the steady sound of the dripping water into the bucket in the bathroom is reassuring.

I have been looking over my list of things to do. How important are they on this leaden day? I study my agenda. There are no doctor's appointments. Grocery? Why do I need to go to the grocery store when there is food in the refrigerator? Drip! Why do I need to go to the quilt store when I already have fabric piled on chairs and couches? Drip! Why do I need to go to the pharmacy when I have vitamins for at least two more days? Drip! The post office? The shoe repair shop? The dry cleaner?

The radio is playing music with a joyful beat. The light in my workroom is warm, bright, and comforting. Drip!

Suddenly, I find that I have made a decision on this miserable, wet, dark day. I have set my priorities. I acknowledge that in life, there are some things that are not important and there are some things that must be done. I understand in my heart that a woman's gotta do what a woman's gotta do, and I'm gonna do it. I'm going to quilt.

HIP! HIP! HOORAY!

WHEN I CAME HOME FROM THE HOSPITAL AFTER getting my new hip, I struggled up the steps with two gorgeous men hauling and pushing me. I waddled in the front door, thumped along with my walker, and trundled into my workroom, where we had set up a bed. After the exciting moment when I backed my hip into the carved footpost of the bed, I dropped onto the bed, flailing about like an up-turned turtle until I had my head at the right end, and pulled up my quilt.

Ordinarily, I would not have been content to lie, in the middle of the day, swaddled in my quilt. Mostly, I over-plan, over-live each day, over-do. I lead a life so busy, in fact, that I had not realized I had a hip problem, until I woke one day and found I could not walk. Since that was unacceptable, I did something about it. The "something" I did was not a cheerful experience. I would rather go to a baseball game, or on a cruise, or to a quilt show.

I came through hospitalization with flying colors, pampered by super-competent medical people and indulged by friends and family. But before I put myself into their hands, I had chosen "the quilt." For many years, I have made bed-sized quilts, meant to be snuggled under. The one I chose for this occasion was a green-and-white Pine Tree quilt. It has a sweet, green gingham back, and diamond blocks break the rigidity

– – – –

of the formal, traditional pine trees. It is soft. I love it, and it loves me ... perfect for cocooning in, for comforting.

Now, only a few days later, I am progressing fabulously. Each night I go to bed, wrapped in my quilt, feeling exhausted and sore. Each morning I wake, a bit stiff and 100 percent improved from the day before. The clue to this is PT (Physical Therapy or Pain and Terror, whichever you prefer). I met a woman recently who has had her new hip for a year, and it has been the worst year of her life. She has, it appears, led a PT less, sedentary year. Yet, I have many friends with bionic hips who could cavort with the best in a very short time after their hip replacements.

The answer to a fast recovery, it seems, is to do those rotten PT exercises. They begin innocuously, with you simply lying stretched out on your bed and wiggling your toes. Then, you work your way through heel slides and fanny tucks. The clincher is the demonic, infamous leg lifts, which I couldn't do even before surgery. You must do 10 of these, lying flat, lifting your leg up, up, pointing to the heavens. You may gasp, moan, yelp, and whimper. Then, you get to roll up in your quilt.

There is a time in all of our lives, when quilts transcend even the wonderment of conceiving and creating them. I have been shown hundreds of ragged quilts that people have explained to me were kept especially to cover them when they were sick children. The patches

- - - -

are worn from fingering, the edges shredded. One quilt of mine is an old Album Quilt, with a butterfly patch that has been reduced to faded threads. Laying that quilt out on the floor and studying it, I have concluded that the butterfly lies exactly where a small child would have grasped and fondled it, perhaps sucking his thumb as he drifted into sleep, comforted.

My Pine Tree Quilt has taken on a new significance for me. Forever after, it will be my Hip Quilt. Long after this soreness has gone and I am dancing in the streets, my quilt will remind me of this comforting. Hooray for my quilt!

IT'S HOW YOU PLAY THE GAME

LUNCH TODAY WAS GOOD. WE HAD HEARTWARMING, homemade chicken soup right out of a box, and crisp, airy popovers, slathered in butter. As we bit into them, the golden melt ran through our fingers and dripped on our chins.

"Aren't they great?" I said.

"They sure are, "said my daughter. "Do you remember the time you made them and they were like hockey pucks?"

"You have a vivid imagination," said I.

"And you have a short memory," she replied.

Here in the North Country every city park has an ice rink in the winter where small boys in enormous padded clothes ricochet back and forth, chasing hockey pucks up and down the ice, whacking them into cages that look like great frames wrapped in fish netting. Hockey pucks are battered, drab objects which, as beauty goes, have no redeeming qualities.

I think I can remember a lot of hockey pucks in my past, those things that started out as a vision, and somewhere along the way turned into objects with no redeeming qualities. The trouble with dealing with hockey pucks is that I never know how to play the game. When I realize that I am struggling with a project that is definitely not doing what it is supposed to be doing, I keep on struggling, knowing that the time I have invested is too valuable to allow me to chuck the project into the

– – – –

nearest waste basket. Sometimes I pick at it and pick at it, undoubtedly making it worse, and certainly tiring it and myself beyond tolerance (which leads to the early aging of both myself and the hockey puck). Sometimes I put it into the box in the corner with all of my other hockey pucks, hoping that time will prove that it is salvageable by some other means.

My box of hockey pucks is in my workroom. There is a pillow in it. The pillow is large and soft and clean. It is also green and maroon. It has a sixteen-piece star in the center and where the points all meet, it has a large, shiny lump. It's too good to throw away. Maybe, on a cold, windy night, some poor soul without a pillow for her head will knock on my door, and I will give her that large, soft, clean pillow, and it will be gone from my life forever.

In my box there is a Hawaiian pillow top that I just don't want to quilt. I love to look at Hawaiian pillows, and someday when life has dealt me a quiet, dull afternoon with nothing in the world to do, I will quilt that pillow around and around and around and I will watch it come to life.

In the box, too, are the parts of two vests, begun for two of my daughters. One is candlewicking for my blind daughter to feel. I was halfway through the candlewicking when I realized that I was using too thick a thread and the knots were coarse and ungainly. The other vest is a blue print fabric of leaves. It was to be a present for my daughter who, at that time, wore long hair and

- - - -

had planned to live out her life in faded jeans. That daughter was married two years ago and now wears shiny hair and ruffly clothes.

There are all of the parts of three wall hangings, the drawings, the fabrics, sitting and waiting. They have been there so long that the inspiration has long since worn off, and I wonder if they really were as marvelous as I thought they would be when the ideas were born.

And there is a computer disk, only two months old, that holds the seed of a quilt that is bumbling around in my head right now.

I dipped into my box of hockey pucks last week and found a piece of a purse that I bought some years ago at a garage sale for 75 cents. It was crazy-pieced and had the embroidery begun. There was a butterfly and a part of a colorful heart, a little fancy stitching and a cherry-red H. I gave it to one of my daughters who happens to be named Helen too, but she gave it back. There it sat and aged in my box. Last week, with a few golden moments on my hands, I decided it was time to whack a hockey puck. I sat each evening, sewing a few more varied stitches along the edges of those patches. At midnight last night I finished my bag.

This morning when I woke, my crazy-quilt bag hung on the door knob. It looked fine. It looked well-shaped, neatly finished. The stitching looked imaginative. A neighbor came by and admired it. Admired? She raved. It looks like I hit that hockey puck a good whack. I scored.

– – – –

MY LIFE DOESN'T ADD UP

I AM BALANCING MY CHECKBOOK! YOU WHO KNOW ME well know that I cry when I balance my checkbook. How can I–who can make geometrics roll over and do tricks–how can I struggle so hard with plain, basic mathematics? I can find my favorite needle in my workroom, but I cannot find that last, miserable penny that is missing in my checkbook.

I am grateful that I have fingers. They are a constant, round number, and they are readily available for use as counters. I can add a sum on my calculator four times, and it will yield four different answers. At least my fingers add up to ten.

Once I went to a Math Trauma Clinic. They said, "Helen. you have a problem." I already knew that I had a problem. They recommended that I take a math course for a cure. My word! Why would I ever want to take a math course? If I were going to study something, I'd study color or design or textiles or history. Those would be better for my heart, and I could use them 365 days a year, not just a couple of dreary days each month.

And so I sit here, bank statement in hand. I have a hot, steaming cup of coffee and a bag of potato chips for solace. Listen! There are small voices calling to me from my workroom. Out there are little pieces of blue and white fabric laid out on my ironing board in a Drunkard's Path. They are beckoning to me. I must be strong. I must be determined. I must resist.

– – – –

I'm coming! I'm coming! Call to me no longer. I'll risk an overdraft fine. I'll balance tomorrow. Today is now. Today I'll stitch my wonderful, wicked Drunkard's Path.

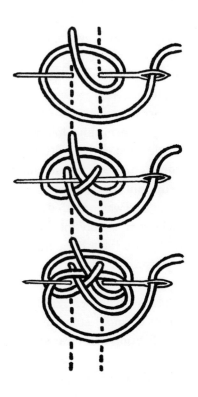

WONDER WOMAN VS. THE WORLD

THE OTHER NIGHT WHEN I WAS RUNNING AN ERRAND, I took a shortcut through the appliance department of my favorite store. I trotted down the aisle and took a left turn at the radios, and suddenly there I was facing the television sets, lined up side by side, bank upon bank, all tuned to the same TV station. The flickering images and bright colors repeated over and over on a multiplicity of glass faces. I was watching the wrestling matches!

As I stood, captured in mid-flight. I saw a giant of a man standing in the ring. He wore black tights, black boots, and a sort of suspender-like black shirt. The muscles in his great arms and enormous chest rippled. His bald head gleamed in the spotlight.

Over the ropes climbed a second giant. This one had on leopard-skin tights and a flowing gold cape. His yellow hair was long and wavy, coiffed as beautifully as any young high school girl ready for the prom. He dropped his cape and the two leviathans hunched their shoulders and circled the ring slowly, facing each other, challenging, surveying.

Suddenly the man in black seized the golden man and gave him a great thump. I stood there watching, fascinated by the realization that I was watching a picture of myself...

There I am, in the center of the ring. I am in my workroom in my pink jogging suit and my Alice-blue track

– – – –

shoes. I am circling. My contender is The World. The World is circling, too. I move closer. I do a few fancy foot movements. I dart back and forth to the kitchen, to the laundry. I sprint to the front door, to the telephone. The World grabs me. I feel the phone bell assaulting my ears. I feel the hot breath of the dryer. The potato peeler raps me on the knuckles.

The referee is shouting at me, scolding me, telling me what I should be doing. Throw him out! Throw the bum out! Out over the ropes!

The aluminum-siding salesman is stomping on my chest. My typewriter has a headlock on me. I shake myself free. My head is swirling, but I recover.

I back into my corner. I breathe deeply. Now, I'm ready for the fight. I charge. Over the side goes The World. There he is, sprawled across the laps of the people in the front row. His priorities and schedules are askew. His calendar is in shambles. Wonder Woman has won! Look at me! I've won! I sit down at my frame in the heat of triumph. Look at me! I've won! I'm quilting!

- - - -

THE STATE OF CIVILIZATION

I AM PROCRASTINATING. BILL AND I ARE SITTING HERE discussing important things, like the condition of the world. "It seems to me," I say, "there are certain behaviors that any civilized person must subscribe to occasionally. First, one must take out the garbage. Second, one must change her underwear from time to time. And third, one must clean the house now and then."

"I think," Bill says, "that two out of three is pretty good."

Since neither of us makes housecleaning a priority, it takes an embarrassingly long time for me to face the fact that this house has been neglected. Occasionally, conscience dictates that I must clean it. The pertinent question is not "Should I?" (yes), or "When?" (now), but "How much?" Most of the job will be pretty easy. I simply will dust everything and vacuum. But I draw the line at washing windows. That is pretty radical behavior. I can, however, satisfy the window challenge by tossing the draperies into the dryer to tumble in some fresh air.

I will fill a bucket with heavy duty cleaner and scrub all of the kitchen, though I think it's not necessary to wipe out the inside of the refrigerator. My trusty little vacuum should pick up the scruffy, dried flakes of onion skins that litter the vegetable bin.

The biggest problem is cleaning my workroom. It has to be somewhat organized just so that I can find things when I want them. I begin by sorting out the debris that

– – – –

I have tacked to my bulletin board. This is where my quilting stencils dangle. Here's a quilting pattern that a friend made for me and a square of fabric that has "1876" woven into the stripes. There are some pewter buttons in the shape of patchwork squares, a snowflake paper cutting, postcards from exotic places, and name tags from quilt conferences. This is really good stuff that I can't possibly throw away. Maybe I will just neaten it.

My pins need to be put back in their separate tins, the fine ones for delicate work, the corsage pins for tacking my quilt to the floor when I baste it, and my big pins with the colored heads for holding my patchwork pieces on my styrofoam wall when I am planning my new quilts. I always intend to sit down with my pliers and straighten out the pins I've bent and warped by sewing over them (I know I shouldn't), but I never seem to get around to it. Pins are not expensive, but salvaging them is just one of those funny economy-type things that I do so that I can spend my money, instead, on fabric. For now, perhaps I will neaten them.

I will, of course, run the vacuum across the carpet. Maybe I will find the quilting needle that I dropped last week. My super-duper cleaning machine makes strange noises when I push it through this room sucking up the miscellany scattered across the floor. It chatters, clanks, rattles, and sometimes it even growls.

I have an astonishing number of rulers propped up between the wall and one of those slotted wooden ruler

– – – –

holders. I bought new rulers when the numbers rubbed off the old ones, but I thought better of tossing out the old ones and kept them. I have lots of 18-inch wooden rulers cut from yardsticks, perfect for drawing straight lines on batting with heavy black markers. The ink from the markers stains the edges of rulers, and if used on plastic ones, the residual ink rubs off onto the fabric. I use these wooden rulers to mark large batts so that I can cut them into smaller pieces. These rulers are important; maybe I will just neaten them.

I have seen all sorts of schemes for disposing of excessive fabric. Some quilters hold garage sales to pare down their stashes, or they donate it for charity quilts. Some cut their fabric into squares and swap them with friends to make charm quilts. When I look at my fabric, I remember that I bought this piece for a special project or fell in love with that piece and just had to have it. I can't discard it. Maybe I will just neaten it up.

My room is overfilled with my treasures, a collection of bits left from a lifetime of quilting encounters. Some people might believe that amassing this assortment of lovingly accumulated loot is uncivilized behavior, beyond the confines of civilized behavior. I must admit, however, that if there had been a quilt shop in ancient Rome, way back when, I would probably have been one of those climbing the walls, ready to pillage and loot with the other barbarians.

– – – –

UP TO MY NECK IN DEEP WATER

I WISH THERE WAS A UNIVERSAL PLUMBING CODE. IT would make me supremely happy if everyone's plumbing were the same. The last time I visited, I struggled to decode my daughter's sink. Do I turn on the water by pulling the knob up or by turning it clockwise? I tried. Finally, I discovered that, if I pulled the knob forward and down, the water would come gushing out.

I spend too much time wrestling with plumbing. If, for instance, there are two handles, is the hot water on the right or the left? I have been alternately scalded and frozen in showers. We had a foreign student "daughter" who took icy cold showers for three months. I thought she liked cold showers. Then, she got the courage to ask us how to turn on the hot water. She would have appreciated universal plumbing.

When we put new faucet handles on our kitchen sink, I told Bill I wanted just the plain, old-fashioned, porcelain, lever-type ones. The kids were charmed with those quaint, simple things. They said they had never seen ones that weren't chrome or fancy plastic faceted globes. I wanted nothing clever, just down-to-earth, turn-the-water-on faucets. Life should always be that simple.

Sewing machines give me the same problems. None of them work the same way, not even those made by the same manufacturer. My little Singer Featherweight threads from right to left. My big, old Singer threads

– – – –

from left to right. My wonderful everyday machine threads from front to back. Sewing machine needles fit into their sockets differently. Bobbins are threaded differently. And running the thread from the spool through the gamut of notches, hooks, and reels is harder to decipher than trying to discover the way to India by sailing around the world. Recently, a quilter told me her machine had no light. We groped and explored her machine for a long time until we finally found the light switch, cleverly hidden away.

I keep the manual for my machine right beneath it. I can piece, since sewing a straight seam is fairly simple. I can even zig-zag without great effort. But when I go adventuring into the incredible array of tensions, stitches, and fancy attachments, I have to sit alone in total silence and study that manual. It is dog-eared now. My machine has become a dear friend and we work together in harmony, but when I go to a workshop, alien machines threaten me. I wish there was a universal sewing-machine code.

I am like Pollyanna, though, and I play the Glad Game. I am glad that we have sewing machines and don't have to sew everything by hand. I am glad that the sewing machine companies are constantly adding new and wonderful innovations. I am glad we have so many options and can choose the machine that fits our needs. I am glad that these machines require so little maintenance

– – – –

when we treat them kindly. I am glad for sewing machines.

My machine is the joy of my life. I use it daily. We have become very close, and I say to it often, "We understand each other so well! Aren't we wonderful together?!" Then, considering how lucky I am to have found this happiness, I add, "Would that the rest of the world were like me and thee."

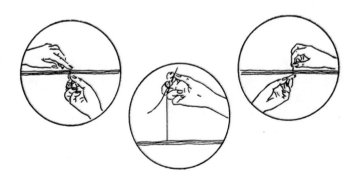

– – – –

SHOWERS OF BLESSINGS

I KNEW EXACTLY WHAT KIND OF SHOWER CURTAIN I wanted when I went to the linen store. I wanted to find one in teal blue brocade to update our 1930s-style green-tile bathroom. I knew that if I could find the proper curtain, it would give dignity and sophistication to our antique inner sanctum.

While I was fingering my way through the display of demure shower curtains, a bright flash of color caught my eye. I flipped back through the pastel draperies to find, nearly buried at the end, a sheet of vinyl with a brilliant flourish of large tropical fish swimming across a swirling, green-blue sea. There were fluorescent teal-colored fish with flashing green tails, round yellow fish with gold stripes, orange fish with black spots, red splotched magenta fish, and blue fish with exotic fins. I had found a glorious shower curtain. It was, in fact, downright funky! I bought it and took it home.

"My," said Bill when he saw it, "that will take some getting used to."

I had visualized my bathroom as a sophisticated, tasteful retreat. Now, instead, it is a whirling sea of excitement. It is not in the least what I had planned. I love it.

This, too, is the story of my quilt life. It rarely goes as planned.

I plan my quilts very carefully before I make them, drawing them out full-sized on a huge piece of white tablecloth paper. My finished quilts, however, never,

– – – –

ever, look like that careful drawing. Somewhere I lose my initial direction, or maybe you can say that I "find" my direction. I rend to make mavericks with minds of their own. My quilts talk to me as I work on them, and I listen to them. I have learned to let them lead me.

The first deviation I make from that carefully drawn picture may come when I go to the store to buy the fabric for this quilt. When I go on a fabric buying spree, images of the perfect materials for my new quilt are vividly etched in my head. I know exactly the colors, the shades, and the kinds of designs I need. But when I get to the shop and look at all those glorious fabrics lined up on the shelves, winking and waving at me, something happens. I discover unique fabrics I hadn't even dreamed of, "just right" sorts of things, wonderful things that tweak my imagination, and instantly the whole personality of my quilt-to-be begins to change. I buy the different, wonderful fabric.

Sometimes, changes will happen when I have cut out all of my pieces and laid them out on the floor to admire them before sewing them together. When I see them there, I discover new possibilities. Other times when I get fabrics laid out in an orderly manner, things are not what they were meant to be. A scrap of material may take on a new personality lying next to bigger, bolder scraps. A tiny triangle of fabric may look quite different from what I saw in a larger piece. Sometimes, a miracle may happen as I work. Odd scraps of fabric may appear in my jumble of materials, and I discover with astonishment that suddenly the unexpected, perfect fabric that I have been looking for has been right there in my stash all along. It's a fascinating game of musical chairs, moving the pieces, changing their places, until they settle into the proper scheme of things.

The size of my quilt may also change. I may make the center of my quilt larger than I had planned because I am pleased with the magic that is happening. Sometimes, I may add fancy borders to make a more glorious quilt. Sometimes I cut off the edges of my quilt, making it smaller and neater. I let the quilt tell me what it wants to be.

When I bought that shower curtain with the tropical fish zinging around it, I took it home, and I hung it in my bathroom. Now, when I stand in my hot, steamy shower with the beads of water glistening across those spectacular fish, I am glad that I listened to my inner voice. What it told me was right. My bathroom needed brightness and joyfulness, not sedate, restrained composure.

I listen to that same inner voice, too, as I am making my quilts, telling me where to make changes, what colors to play with, and how to be free and inventive. I have learned to trust it and let it lead me. I let that voice sort out my loves and my fancies. I listen when it encourages me. Every one of us has a secret voice. If each of us listens and believes, we will make quilts that are—heart and soul—all our very own, and that, Dear One, is the blessing of quiltmaking.

– – – –

THREAD SALES IN THE SUNSET

I AM AN INCURABLE DREAMER. I DREAM THE IMPOSSIBLE dream. When I pass signs tacked to telephone poles at the corners of the streets, I always slow my car. I am hypnotized by them. There are signs for garage sales and yard sales, giant sales and porch sales, moving sales and estate sales. I edge over against the curb and mosey around the corner. Rather than invite a traffic disaster, I let the other cars mutter past me. Then I scutter back to the telephone pole and note the address on the lettered cardboard. It beckons to me like a siren's song.

It's my dream that someday I will happen into one of those sales, those displays of assorted discards, and there winking at me from under a pile of old bedding will be The Quilt. It will be a treasure that is beautifully stitched. Perhaps it will be a Rose of Sharon or a Princess Feather. Maybe a Delectable Mountain. Something absolutely smashing—and I will discover it.

In reality I know that such is not my destiny. Nevertheless, I keep hearing about great finds. One friend found the complete set of patterns from the Rose Wilder Lane *American Needlework* book at a garage sale. Another quilt friend discovered two real, honest-to-goodness Seminole skirts at a flea market. Joyce Aufderheide found a marvelous old quilt in the bottom of a barrel.

Optimist that I am, I find myself cruising past open garage doors, hoping to find my pot of gold at the end of

– – – –

the alley. I search, even though I know for a fact that if there really is a wonderful garage-sale quilt for me to find, you will have bought it first, just before I get there.

NO STRINGS ATTACHED

THIS AFTERNOON I HAVE BEEN TAKING MY "FANKLE" apart, bit by bit. A fankle is what Scottish needleworkers call a snarly nest or mess. Until I met people who do large, lovely counted thread pictures and keep their flosses in controlled assortments, I thought that everyone's embroidery threads were in a fankle.

I am making pansies for the bottom of my latest quilt, and I want to embellish them with embroidered little purple lines in their centers. I found a lovely length of deep purple thread in my fankle, and bit by bit, inch by inch, I worked it out of the wad. As I untwisted the threads, I remembered doing the same thing as a little girl when we played with marionettes. I would guess that I spent nearly half the playtime untangling the strings of those puppets. I did not realize then what good training this would be for my later years.

Once I had extracted my purple floss, I was inspired to move on. My other threads are in a similar state. A collection of quilting threads is displayed on a board hanging on the wall of my workroom. Sewing threads are arranged in clear plastic boxes stacked nearly three feet high on the bookshelf. Odds-and-ends threads, including ancient spools of silks and metallics, are hidden away in a little wicker basket, and threaded sewing machine bobbins have their own special box beside my work. My whites and blacks are filed in the lid of a shoe

– – – –

HELEN KELLEY'S

box in my tool cupboard drawer. All of these hidey places have masses of thread ends spewing from them. Either the spools have unwound, or I never quite got the loose ends hooked into the notches on the rims of the spools in the first place.

To clean up these messes, I gave each thread collection a hair cut. I simply took my scissors and snipped off the mazes of loose threads. They look lovely now, all disciplined and neat, and I feel a heady success.

In this frenzy of neatness, I find myself looking for more scruffy fibers. Perhaps I could neaten up my fabric. My stash is quite hairy because it scraggles the ravelings of gangly threads that shredded along the edges of each piece when I prewashed it before I put it away. I know that I should serge or pink or nip the raw edges before I drop the material into the washer, but I have never been that well organized.

I believe there is something deeply philosophical about my loose ends. If you are like me, you may find yourself asking, "Is this a reflection of my life? Am I destined to spend my life in a cosmic fankle dealing with lint and shreds, forever neatening things, snipping, and vacuuming? As a quilter who is litter-prone, can I untangle my life?"

A LITTLE SOMETHING
WORTH MENTIONING...

FOR THE LAST THREE NIGHTS, I HAVE ROAMED AROUND this dark house in the wee hours, wakened around 2 A.M. by a faint sound, a gentle "beep."

A year ago, we installed new smoke alarms in the ceiling of every room and armed them with shiny, vigorous, new batteries. Now, one year later, those batteries are dying, all at the same time, or at least one alarm each on successive nights. The first night, Bill found me sitting at the top of the stairs listening intently in the dark, trying to determine which fixture needed attention. The second night, I shut the bedroom door and simply sealed out the steady, demanding, annoying beep. The third night, I got up and moved my pillow down to the living room couch. That day Bill simply took out all of the batteries in all of the alarms and replaced them. Now they are fresh and new again, until next year.

Waiting in the dark, listening to those beeps, waiting, waiting for the next one, and the next, was torture. Little things can certainly get your attention.

Have you noticed how many little things are clamoring for your attention when you are making a quilt? I think, for instance, of the times when I've been quilting, and I discover a broken thread or an errant knot or a pencil mark somewhere in the middle of that vast

– – – –

sea of fabric. It's tempting to leave it for later, but if I put off fixing it, I will never find it again, until my quilt is hung in a show. Hanging in the show, I discover where that pencil mark or knot is, right there at eye level. Naturally it will be hung with a spot light on it to make it easier for me—and the rest of the world—to see.

Little things can be good, too. Don't misunderstand me. How many times have you looked at a quilt in a show that may, at first, seem quite usual, and wondered what there is about it that catches your attention, that makes it a winner? It may be made from a familiar old pattern, but like a favorite friend, there is something out-of-the-ordinary about it such as a wonderful use of color, or a subtle embellishment. As gentle as that little touch is, it has transformed a prosaic quilt into something unique.

Sometimes, little things are simple and personal. I have my scissors, my quilting needles, and my thimble right here by my frame. When I sit down to work, my lights are just the way I like them, my iron is in place, my sewing machine is just right, and my usual radio station is playing beside me. To anyone else, this might seem inconsequential, but all of these little details give me a big feeling of comfort.

Each big thing in our lives is a composite of everyday, little things. We choose which of these to embrace and which one to overlook. Dust motes in my home

– – – –

don't bother me. A few dirty dishes in the sink can wait until I have accumulated enough to make it worthwhile to stop and wash them. These little moments I ignore. Important in my life are sharp pins, matching threads, and small golden moments. These are little things that mean so much.

CRAZINESS

I AM SITTING HERE, SEWING SEQUINS ON A DRESS. THE morning is lovely, and the light is golden. I have fabric sorted and piled neatly and pattern pieces arranged, and I would rather be quilting! Instead, I sit here beneath a strong lamp, with a spool of black thread and a dress that is covered with straggling black sequins and dangling threads.

My granddaughter is going to be in a parade. Because it will be a nighttime extravaganza, sequins that sparkle in the street lights are *de rigueur.* She was given this dress as a gift, and it is unwearable. With each movement, the sequins flutter off and sprinkle like snow flakes. The lining bulges below the hemline, and if I pick out and reset the edges to match, more sequins will straggle loose. The placket does not match because the hooks and eyes are skewed. I am tucking, overcasting, and securing loose threads, and I am scavenging rogue sequins and beads and tacking them in empty spots. The dress was obviously made by an unskilled seamstress. As I said before, I would rather be quilting.

The sequins were sewn in place with a chain-stitch machine. I am all too familiar with the advantages and pitfalls of the chain stitch. When I was a small child, I learned to sew on my mother's old Wilcox and Gibbs chain-stitch sewing machine. It had been "modernized," removed from its tiny treadle stand and electrified. Mother set the machine on her dressing-table bench for me, and I sat in front of it in a child-size chair. I learned that, if I caught the loose chain loop at the end of the seam, in one movement, I could quickly and easily pull out an entire length of bad stitching. I also learned that, if I did nor carefully knot off that loose loop, I could just as easily pull out an entire length of a good seam.

So it is with sequins that are sewn in place with a chain stitch. A tug of one dangling thread that has not been secured, and sequins will burst off the dress like peas from a pea shooter. Starting at the bottom of the dress, and working up, inch by inch, I am searching for un-secured threads. I tug. I test. I catch the knots. Threading the loose threads into a darning needle, I push the needle, eye first, between the layers of dress and lining to hide the scruffy ends. The vulnerable areas seem to move ahead of me, multiplying and threatening. More and more dribbling sequins need to be reapplied. I'd rather be quilting.

As I sit here, squinting, searching, and stitching, my mind wanders. I remember back to the time I agreed to repair an aged crazy quilt. It had been a lovely quilt, painted, embroidered, and of course, made of silks that were crumbling. When my friend brought me the quilt, I laid it out on my table under a strong light, and care-

– – – –

fully examined it. "It looks," I said, "as if there are about three places that need to be protected." I calculated that I could easily fix her quilt in a day. It would need a few darning stitches and a bit of netting tacked in place.

I discovered that the damage in the fabric on the crazy quilt seemed to move just ahead of me, breaking and sighing, no matter how gently I worked. As I handled it, I could hear the fragile threads crying, and I realized that I could work forever on the quilt and I would never be done. I was working on an eternal project.

This sequined dress is an eternal project. It is impossible to make the dress perfect. There is no way that I can hide every vagrant thread, stitch every insecure bead, or tuck every gap and bulge. I have worked all day on this dress, and yet, I could not guarantee that, when my granddaughter puts it on, she would not be showered with loose sequins.

As it was with that quilt, when is the time to stop? Is this the moment to lay down my needle and say, "Enough"? Will there ever be an end to the project?

The big question is this: When does a sequined dress become lunacy, and when does a damaged quilt become crazy?

CHAPTER 4
Words By Which to Sew a Stitch

WORDS TO LIVE BY

A CROSS-STITCHED SAMPLER HANGS ON THE WALL IN my downstairs bathroom. It's garish in its lavender frame, and I laugh when I see it because I know that when I die, an estate-sales person will come into my house and sell that picture for an antique. Perhaps, since I sewed it when I was in high school, it may very well be an antique by the time I am gone.

My sampler has a garland of embroidered flowers across the top and across the bottom, and in between, in large rosy block letters, it reads "LORD, HELP ME TO KEEP MY BIG MOUTH SHUT."

I read this sampler daily and I recite it like a litany, over and over to myself. It does no good. I get very excited about things. I am a creature of the moment, and I tend to blather without thinking. My more sophisticated friends speak in well-modulated voices, and they say considered things of great import. I have resolved that I will read my sampler every morning and imprint it upon my brain so that I can try to keep my comments on any one subject controlled and thoughtful.

If a quilter shows me a quilt, newly finished, and it is absolutely wonderful, I must not gush. I will not go into raptures. I will make only pertinent, calculated comments that are thoughtful and appropriate. Otherwise, *Lord, help me to keep my big mouth shut.*

– – – –

If I am shown a quilt that has been labored over long with fingers pricked, threads scattered, and it comes from the very heart of its maker, but the color is not quite the color I would prefer, or the edges are not quite as straight as I could wish, *Lord, help me to keep my big mouth shut.*

If I am standing at the counter at the fabric store, and the lady in front of me is struggling with a fabric decision, and she doesn't ask me for my help, *Lord, help me to keep my big mouth shut.*

If I am standing in an elevator and someone gets on wearing an absolutely marvelous piece of quilted clothing, and she doesn't know me from Adam, I must not embarrass this stranger. *Lord, help me to keep my big mouth shut.*

If I go to a meeting and hear two people who are seated behind me discussing highly personal problems like families who are upset about things like pins in the carpet or too many microwave dinners, and no one asked me for my opinion, *Lord, help me to keep my big mouth shut.*

There are things in this world that are none of my business. Nobody asked me my opinion! I must learn to be discrete, courteous, and to keep quiet. If you do ask me, however, and you have something wonderful or intriguing or exciting—if you *do* ask me, then I don't need to keep my big mouth shut.

– – – –

MY STARS!

YESTERDAY WAS AN AUSPICIOUS DAY. GENERALLY AM not an advocate of astrology, though I confess that every week I turn to the horoscope in the Sunday paper. If it says something encouraging, I am delighted. If I read a warning, I chuckle at its naiveté and go about my life unthreatened. However, during the last twenty-four hours I am sure that an astrologer would have discovered that all of my stars were lined up in the sky magnificently, rising and falling in the proper order. They must have been winking and glowing benignly. My Taurus the Bull must surely have been trotting through his celestial pasture, gently flicking his tail, lowing softly, and nuzzling at the Gemini Twins. I need to commemorate the day.

Just twenty-four hours ago, I awoke. It was still night and I discovered that I was wide awake. No sense in just lying there. So I got up. I flicked on the light in my workroom and picked up my scissors. I laid out my newly washed fabric for a friendship quilt. With the selvedge trimmed away, it was exactly the width of three blocks. There was not an inch wasted. The grain was perfect, running true and even. There were no flaws, no nicks. When the sun came up, I had thirty good blocks neatly stacked, ready to mail out. I had figured the material exactly, so there would be no return trips to the fabric store to find just a little bit more, and no waste, either.

– – – –

Old Taurus must have smiled and sniffed the cosmic flowers.

I ate a little breakfast and resisted the extra cup of coffee I shouldn't have. I went back to work. The sun shone. I stitched on my new pieced quilt. The sewing machine hummed. The phone rang a few times, just to let me know that people "cared." The conversations were pleasant and brief. I was even able to stop the roofing salesman midsentence. I firmly told him "Not today," and astonishingly he didn't argue.

The family drifted in and out. They chatted as I worked. Nobody had to be anywhere frantically. My sewing machine hummed on. My quilt pieces fit together perfectly. My starry Taurus must have munched gently on a few tufts of soft grass.

By the time I had worked my way to four o'clock, I had piled up pieced strips of neatly pressed pieces, each fitting crisply into the other, their edges smooth, points together. I felt accomplished. I would cook something creative. This was the time to tackle that new recipe for ratatouille. I chopped and pared efficiently. I sauteed expertly. I seasoned magnificently. Usually, at best, I cook adequately, but this concoction was food for a king. It was done, not only on time, but fifteen minutes early. When I called, everyone came to the table. My husband even abandoned "Barney Miller" at the midpoint. Nobody asked me what was in my ratatouille so I didn't have to tell them, "eggplant." They licked their plates. They followed me to the sink, scraping their dishes with their spoons to get the last bits. My husband volunteered to do the dishes!

Back I went to the ironing board to touch up a bit more of my piecing. Old Taurus was getting tired. He was slowing down a bit. I sorted through fabric and folded it. Taurus stretched out in the heavenly grass, contented. I began to feel as limp as a forgotten piece of week-old lettuce in the bottom of the refrigerator. My family was busy doing family-type things as I found my way up to bed. Poor, tired Taurus. He slumbered, feet up in Elysian meadows, with visions of calico flowers dancing through his head.

It is just twenty-four hours later. I have no desire to get up and work. I am content to lie and watch the shadows on the wall. Shortly it will be dawn again. The alarm will ring. My first cup of coffee will probably drip on the rug. The dog will thump me as she pushes out of the door for her morning constitutional. I will discover that we are all out of orange juice. Taurus will stretch, maybe even snort a little. He will rise to his feet and arch his neck. He will stamp his hooves, and he will begin this new day by plodding determinedly back into his usual stubborn path across the sky.

- - - -

SEA SIGHS

FOR AWHILE, I LIVED ON AN ISLAND IN THE SEA. WHEN Bill was in the service, we made our home in a beach house on one of the islands of the Outer Banks of North Carolina.

Fall, winter, and early spring are not tourist time in this part of the world. It's a time of solitude. Late fall is damp, and in the morning you wake and realize that the world is very cold. As winter sets in, you turn on your heater and wrap your body in warm clothes against the wind. You also discover some quite wonderful things.

Living in a beach resort through the winter is an isolated life. The few people who remain close their doors to the cold, but, in that quiet, insular time, there is a pleasant sense of seclusion. Your days become secure in the rhythm of the sea. Every day the tide rises and falls. The sound of the breakers never stops, not for a single breath of a moment. The wind blows steadily. There is a reliable, comforting consistency to life on an island in winter.

I learned some lessons about living while I was on that island. I learned to listen to the regulated wash of the waves. I learned, when I stepped into the salty gust of briny air, to breathe deeply and savor it. I learned, while walking the wet, sandy beach at low tide, to focus my eyes, to scan the ground ahead of me, to discover treasures, simple ones tumbled and tossed up by the waves because with every tide, there is newness.

- - - -

When I sit alone and quilt, I have found these same pleasures. My eyes drift across my quilt, looking for the simple gifts, the fabric rising and falling evenly, breathing an elegance into the flat plane of the quilt top.

I find that as I work, I am absorbed in my thoughts, in the rhythm of my world. I wonder if the movement of my quilting hand steadily rocking against the quilt top is not akin to the repeating motion of the waves. Quilting, too, is comforting.

In March and April, spring comes to the ocean. As you walk the beach, you discover new life washing ashore. Birds soar over the breakers with a fresher, braver demeanor. The sun shines brighter. The air smells warmer. The feeling is much the same as when one discovers that her quilt is nearly born. The moment is a prelude to a joyful happening. Looking at an almost finished quilt, you see its loveliness as it swells and dips in patterns of grace. The nearly finished quilt is filled with promise.

In the stillness of my workroom, bending over my quilt in the gentle, quiet moments of the day, I realize what a gift the sea gave me by showing me how to savor small things. It taught me to enjoy rhythm and movement, to find comfort in the dependable moments, and to take great pleasure in watching the patterns of life unfold.

– – – –

THURSDAY'S CHILD

"GUESS WHAT," BILL SAID, "YOU WERE BORN ON A THURSDAY."

Some husbands buy golf clubs. Some buy motorcycles. My husband is addicted to buying odd computer programs of little or no value. He had been playing with a program that he found in a sale bin at our local computer store. It will give you irrelevant information about any date you put into its maw. As far as I can figure, the program must have data all the way back to Year One. So far, Bill has regressed to 1889.

Some years ago, at a quilt conference, I bought a set of greeting cards that are reproductions of antique trade cards. The original cards were printed by a thread company around 1888. Each one has a child pictured on it and a line of that old poem about the attributes of children according to the day of the week on which they were born. I was curious about what kind of things might have been said about me, born on a Thursday. A search through the debris on my desk produced the package of cards tucked neatly away behind a deck of file cards and some sticky note paper. I fingered through the pictures of sweet Victorian children. Among the accompanying quotes, I found that Monday's child is fair of face, Tuesday's child is full of grace, and that Wednesday's child is merry and glad. "Ah, ha," I thought. "Here is Thursday."

- - - -

"Thursday's child is sour and sad!" Good heavens! Sour and sad!

"You had to find out, didn't you? Your curiosity got the best of you, and you had to know!" said Bill.

He's right. I am like Rudyard Kipling's elephant's child, that little creature with the "insatiable curiosity" who went about poking his snub-nose into other people's business until the crocodile grabbed hold of his little short nose and pulled and pulled, and finally it became a very, very long nose. I have a curiosity like the elephant's child.

I think it was my curiosity that first got me interested in quilting. My mother's best bedspread was a beautiful quilt with the roses sewn in place with meticulous, tiny buttonhole stitches of rose-colored floss. I grew tip with that quilt always spread out on the bed in our guest room. Somewhere along the way to growing up, I became curious about it. It drove me into a frenzy of reading about quilt history, rifling through the library to discover facts about the how and when of sateen fabric, the process of stitching quilt layers together, and the lives of quilt-makers in the 1920s. I was off and running on a restless and relentless search for information about quiltmaking. Because I am curious, I have stuffed notebooks full of material over the years. I have not the faintest idea what I shall do with that material, but those articles are filled with facts that I thought I needed to know.

– – – –

Perhaps it is a good thing to be a quilter who is curious. Other quilters ask me questions. They want to know what batting I use, or how many stitches I take, or what kind of fabric I prefer. All of that is trivia, but finding the answers to questions that lurk in one's head is satisfying. Strangely enough, I find myself asking these very same questions of other quilters I meet. Collectively, we are building a mental reference library of useful facts and trivial information.

When I read the Sunday paper, I usually flip through the pages to the entertainment section and read the horoscopes. I am especially fond of fortune cookies, too. It's great fun to test our perceptions of ourselves against the whimsical proclamations of The Fates, who happen to be people who know nothing about us, really. I can chant that old poem, too, about the charming attributes of pretty children (all except Thursday's child), but I refuse to believe that anything about our lives is set in stone. If you just look at the facts, I am sure that you will find Thursday's children throughout history have been charming, intelligent, and clever.

Therefore, Merry and glad, Wednesday's child may be, But Thursday's is blest with curiosity.

BITTERSWEET

THE SUMMER THAT I WAS 12 YEARS OLD, MY FRIENDS and I formed a club. Four of us girls, all the same age, lived in adjacent houses on the same block. We called ourselves "The Happy Helpers," and my mother made us a club flag out of a piece of old sheet appliqued with a big, red "H." Our organization was exactly right. Since there were just four of us, each of us got to be an officer: president, vice president, treasurer, and secretary. The meetings went without a flaw. First, we saluted the flag, and since we had no money and no minutes, we ate. Someone's mother provided lemonade and cookies. It was a good club.

I can remember that we did two things in our club. We spent our sunny days in Priscilla Brewster's backyard. It was an ideal place, hidden behind the garage and shielded by tall lilac bushes. There, we worked at building a clubhouse. My father was employed at the time by a building supplies manufacturer, and so he brought us the clubhouse materials knotty wood, warped boards, bent nails, and a large roll of tar paper. We dug holes, put in corner posts and hammered boards and tar paper to the sides. We worked hard on our clubhouse during the daylight hours. Every night, the neighborhood boys tore it down. Every day, we built it back again.

On rainy days, we sewed on our uniforms. We had chosen a Hollywood pattern that cost 15 cents, and there was a movie star's picture on the pocket. The dresses were bright blue with white collars and cuffs, and they had belts with shiny red celluloid buckles. The material for my dress came from the basement of the local five-and-dime store. I learned more about sewing when I was making that dress than I had ever learned before or since. My uniform was a work of art. It had perfect buttonholes, done by hand. I still have a picture of myself as I posed proudly in my brand-spanking-new dress, all crisp and neat.

I learned another lesson that summer, one that I vividly remembered the other day as I was working on my quilt. The lesson was a bitter one. Back in that summer of 1939, after I had worn my new uniform to my first club meeting, my mother washed it. That bright blue dye ran all over those pristine white collars and cuffs. It was impossible to salvage my dress. All of my pride, my excitement, my pleasure was washed away in that swirling blue, blue water. The depth of my despair over that ruined dress is beyond description. The other day, when I was finishing my quilt, I came close to experiencing that feeling again.

- - - -

I had done everything exactly right on my quilt. It was sewn, quilted, bound off, and signed. I had the ultimate satisfaction of standing back to see my finished work as the quilt lies even, the edges straight, the knots snapped inside, the colors just right, the points meeting perfectly, and the appliqué rounded and smooth.

I was smug with satisfaction. Then, I noticed a marked quilting line that I had not removed. I scrubbed the quilt with an eraser, but the mark was stubborn. I mixed a soap and water solution and dabbed it on the pencil mark. I worked a bit of the soapy water into the quilt. The pencil mark stayed, but the green color in the fabric began creeping out into the surrounding white fabric. I turned the quilt over and found a green blot beginning to stain the backing. I wrung out my rag and tried to stroke the stain evenly to blend in. "Perhaps," I thought, "if the coloring is even, people will think it's part of the design."

What an absurd thought! Obviously, the green dye had run. That old feeling of horror settled over me. I was twelve years old again, watching helplessly as all my labor and all of my love was being ruined by an ugly stain.

I worked over that green blot, stroking it gently with my damp cloth. Using a strong light to see better, I clipped threads and eased out the edge of the appliqué to cover the stain a bit. I struggled. I stitched. I think I fixed it. If I showed it to you now, you would probably

– – – –

not see that stain. The damage seems to have been softened enough to fool the unsuspecting eve.

It's strange how the little things from our childhood, the exuberant joys, the gentle pleasures, and the sadnesses come back to us years later. This time. I am older and perhaps more skillful. I have salvaged my quilt, but the little moments of our lives repeat themselves, and sometimes now, as adults, quite unexpectedly we taste again those poignant memories.

QUOTH THE RAVEN

MY SISTER, NANCY, HAD A CROW. AS HER CHILDREN WERE growing up, her family took in and sheltered lots of orphaned animals. There was a calf named Kelley who drank his milk from a baby's bottle, and a chicken named Cluck-Cluck who nestled contentedly in the crooks of children's arms. Another one of the creatures was Goosey-Loosey, who disqualified herself from the judging at the county fair when she ate her own registration tag.

My favorite, by far, was Crow. He lived a king's life, ruling the backyard from a large mesh cage. The neighborhood kids would bring him lovely tidbits to eat, and he was taken on trips to schools and summer camps where he always posed and preened his glossy black and purple feathers in the glow of childhood admiration.

Great, raspy croaks emanated from Crow's cage in the backyard when he woke from a snooze and stretched his wings. Occasionally, Crow would screech. He would shout something in a strange, garbled language. No one could decipher it. Crow would call, "Ar-I-so-wa!" Several times a day that bird cried, "Ar-I-so-wa!"

One hot day, as Nancy was working feverishly in the kitchen over a large family banquet, her youngest son banged on the screen door.

"Mama, Jeffery hit me!" he wailed.

"All right. So what?" Nancy answered.

"Ar-I-so-wa!" echoed the crow.

- - - -

We howled with laughter. It was in that moment that we understood what Crow had been saying all those years. How many times had he repeated that phrase as it filtered through the back-door screen to a fretting child?

That crow call echoes through my head almost daily, especially when I am making a quilt. I tend to fuss over my sewing. The hours slip by as I agonize over two shades of rose or lavender. I wrestle in my sleep over those decisions that I have struggled with unsuccessfully at bed time, and I get up before dawn to make minute changes. In other words, I am a nit-picker.

The one leveling influence that I have in my life is Crow, echoing again in my head. As I struggle with my choices, I hear him cry out to me, "Ar-I-so-wa!"

Sometimes these tiny decisions don't make a fig of a difference. Sometimes, two shades of the same color look identical when they are sewn into a quilt. Sometimes, even if they are different, either will work. Sometimes now, when I reach the stage where I am frantically wrestling with my options, I say to myself, "Ar-I-so-wa!" Then, I write the choices down on pieces of paper and put them behind my back. I shuffle them, and whichever one comes 'round in my right hand is the one I use. Months later, weeks later, even days later, I rehash the situation, and I cannot imagine why I had struggled so to make the decision. Sometimes,

- - - -

tiny differences are important, and sometimes they are not.

A quilter could go goofy with all of her options—color, shape, width of borders, fabric, quilting design. I once knew a man whose philosophy was that a person has only so many decisions to make in a lifetime, and he said he was saving his decisions for the important moments. With a doctrine like that, one would be awash in a perpetual sea of uncertainty. Procrastination will not make a quilt.

Each step in making a quilt, from the starting moment to the last stitch in the binding, is a choice, and that's what makes a quilt so personal and so satisfying. Some decisions are important; some aren't. We need to be able to define which problems are worth stewing over. If you are a quiltmaker like me, a fussbudget, worry-wart sort of person, perhaps you will find some relief, too, by letting Crow's echo play around in your head.

When you are drowning in fabric choices and pattern options, ask yourself in simple, everyday English, "Ar-I-so-wa?"

Quoth the Raven evermore!

– – – –

A FABLE

THERE WERE TWO BIRDS CAUGHT IN THE CHIMNEY. FOR three days they fluttered, beating their wings frantically against the walls of the flue. I sat and sewed and listened. How long can a bird live without water or food or hope? I worried about those birds as I stitched and listened. I tried opening the fire screen, and then I opened the damper a tiny bit to see if they would come into the fireplace. One bird dropped down through the opening and scuttled beneath the andirons. I poked at it with a yardstick to rout it out, and it darted out across the hearth, eluding my waiting butterfly net. I chased it, dashing from room to room, swooping my butterfly net to catch it. It flew headlong into a window. It flitted past my head and skittered to a stop on the top of the bookcase, strewing feathers. It dove down and settled on my thread case. It sat there and huddled. It darted and dove again, and I chased it. Finally, exhausted, it settled on my sewing box. I dipped the net around it and freed it through the back door. It soared off into the trees with battered feathers, disheveled but safe.

The second bird was still in the chimney. I opened the damper wider and waited. Surely, I thought, this bird would understand that I was friendly and that it should come down to be captured and set free, too. The moments ticked by. Finally, the little bird dropped down into the fireplace and settled on the tip of the andiron. As I positioned the butterfly net, the bird fluttered

– – – –

briefly, and then gently, gracefully, as if by magic, it rose on the warm updraft that lifted from the room up through the flue, and it floated upwards gracefully, up and out. Quite simply, quite miraculously, it was free.

I've been working on a problem. I've cut little quilt shapes from colored paper and laid them out on the floor to help me plan my next quilt. I've moved them around and rearranged them in a variety of configurations. I've cut more pieces, new ones of different colors. I've added new shapes. Feeling stalemated, I've walked away and had a phone conversation and drunk a cup of coffee. I stopped once and did a crossword puzzle, trying to clear my mind of the obsession.

I have beaten my wings and flittered and struggled for two days now. Last night, as I lay in my bed, the shapes and colors played across my mind. I fell asleep, and still they played and fluttered. This morning, I found that I was no closer to solving my problem.

Now, I have thrown away all those little, intricate pieces with oblique angles and clever joinings. I chose a single, simple shape. Next, I picked out a few of my favorite colors and eliminated those dozens of tints and shades. Using the simple shape and those few colors, I have laid the new quilt shapes out on the floor. I like what I see. It is simple. It is refreshing. It is pleasant to work with. It is flutter-free. This is a quilt that is going to be pure pleasure to make. *Moral:* Sometimes we try too hard. Sometimes *easier* is *better.*

– – – –

MY REFUGE, AND MY STRENGTH

WE ARE DOING SOME REMODELING WORK ON THE HOUSE, and today they are fixing that small area of the roof above my workroom where the bay window will be inserted to open up and dispel the gloom in the upstairs hall. I am sitting here quilting. I may look strange, however, as I am hunched over my quilting frame with two lamps casting a lovely, golden light across my work. The curtains are open, too, to let in the sun. All of that is not so unusual, but on my head is a pair of those giant, plastic ear-muffy things that the runway workers at the airport wear to buffer the sound from the screaming jet engines.

Directly above my head is a flat roof, and onto it, the roofers are dropping giant rolls of tar paper. They are tromping over my head like flamenco dancers, their stomping heels beating a staccato chorus with their flailing hammers.

Bill came down and set these soundproof mufflers over my ears, and the level of noise dropped to that of chickens scratching. Now I sit in splendid quiet, untouched by the chaos above me, and I quilt. I am bending over my frame as I work, and it is as if I am protecting my quilt from the turmoil. This is the first time that I have ever had to shelter my quilting. Usually my quilting shelters me.

It's a strange phenomenon that when events make me tense and things need doing, I quilt. Quilting calms

- - - -

me and gives me a chance to reflect and sort out my life. Concentrating on those little stitches, solving the puzzles of depth and dimension, and feeling the fabric all help me to see more clearly. With only a few moments of medicinal quilting, I can be ready to tackle the world's problems.

My sister commented to me last night that she didn't understand why I was celebrating the fact that I have a new quilt in the frame. She supposed, she said, that quilting must be boring. Quilting is not boring. Quilting is that still space in my life surrounded by daily uproar. If a symphony were all raucous crescendos or a picture were painted in total highlights, it could never be appreciated, its concepts never understood. The quiet spots, the gentle moments underscore the elegance. My quilting is a soft, sweet moment that gives me the grace to appreciate the tumultuous times. It shelters me.

This afternoon the workmen will tear a hole in the back of our house to make it ready for that new bay window with a deep sill where I can put my potted flowers in the winter. It will be noisy again. The sound of splintering boards and squealing nails being pulled from their holes should create a bedlam, but I will bend over my quilt frame again, wearing my ear protectors, and quilt in a satisfying solitude. My quilting is my refuge.

– – – –

MY HEART LEAPS UP

BEFORE DAWN THIS MORNING I WOKE AND PACKED THE car for my return trip from my guild's big quilt-affair. As I headed southwest, the sun broke across the horizon and blazed in my rearview mirror. The sky turned blue, and I could see fluffy clouds. Pillows of fog drifted above the shady pockets of the woods along the side of the road.

The fog whiffs burned away, and I noticed that my windshield was decorated with stray, straggly leaves and a nick from a flying cinder. The glass had a strange luminous spot on it. Perhaps, I thought, it was the sunlight breaking through and refracting from the flaw. As I drove, the color of the sky deepened, and the glow spot on my windshield began to grow. Slowly, the sky turned a haunting, leaden indigo. The single glow of color turned into a spear of colored light. The fluorescence of it grew as I watched it reach up into the heavens.

Suddenly, against the depths of darkness, it arched into a spectacular double rainbow, spanning from horizon to horizon. The glory of it made me gasp, and at that same moment, a torrent of dark rain spattered across the car.

The rainbow melted into the liquid turbulence.

I sat in the car, pelted by the gloom of the storm, but the opulence of the rainbow still filled me. It scintillated. It was the essence of everything I had ever learned

- - - -

about color, its emotion, its satisfaction, and its excitement. That rainbow, that mystery that dazzling color is still printed on my mind.

Color is a gift. The brilliance and depth of the hues of the fabrics on our store shelves, waiting for us to sample and taste and then take home for a textile banquet, is a deep-down joy. Those tints and shades that we sort through and stitch into our quilts beguile us: Playing with color, drinking it in, listening to it, and feeling it is a satisfaction. Indeed–*indeed*–color is a gift.

Recently I planned to make a quilt for a friend as an anniversary present. I asked her, "What are your favorite colors?"

"Oh, just black and white," she said. "Everything I own is black and white."

My heart sank. Her black and white anniversary quilt was going to look more like an obituary than a blessing. Surely, I thought, I had to use some color. I would stitch in some sort of light, some brilliance and excitement. To the black and white quilt, I added two simple red butterflies. Those brightly colored butterflies soar on that quilt just as that rainbow soared against the indigo sky. Color added emotion. Color is a gift.

The poet William Wordsworth understood about beholding rainbows. The colors of the rainbow touched the depths of my heart, and just as he says, they made my heart leap up!

– – – –

FOLLOWING THE THREAD
OF THE STORY

HERE'S A WEIRD STORY FOR YOU! I THOUGHT I'D SEEN lots happen in this quilting thing we do, but I've never seen this one before. It all began with a telephone call from my daughter, Jo. I could hear the horror in her voice. "What's the matter?" I asked her.

She had been putting together a wonderful pieced quilt with peachy stars on a royal blue-and-white background. It was nearly finished the last time she showed it to me. She'd made the points and joinings perfectly. It lay flat and even. The two shades of peach created a delicate transparency.

"Mom," she said, "You know this enormous quilt that I've been making for a wedding gift? I just picked up the top, and it came to pieces in my hands. The whole quilt is disintegrating!"

"Stay calm," I said. "Let's back up and see if we can figure out what has happened in the piecing process. What kind of thread are you using?"

"It's stuff that I had here in the house. It's the thread on the big cardboard cone."

"It's serger thread," I said. "It's a polyester monofilament. Did you press your piecing with a hot iron?"

"Oh, yes," she said wearily. "I was very careful. I wanted it to be perfect."

Jo had melted the thread in her quilt with the heat of

– – – –

her iron. In some places it had disappeared into the fabric, and in others, it had fused in globs.

"Hold on, I'm coming out," I said.

"No," she said. "It's my problem, and it's my responsibility."

I went anyway.

I found Jo in her sewing room surrounded with peachy stars and blue-and-white inserts in various stages of falling apart. Separating blocks were piled on the bed. Triangles littered the floor. We collected the pieces in piles, and began the picking apart and resewing of the starry quilt.

Serger thread is handy. I use serger thread too, but not for permanent seams. I use it for basting. It breaks away easily, and it's cheap. It's perfect for holding things together temporarily. When I use it in our dry climate, it clings and crackles with electricity. You can tell clearly when I am basting with serger thread; I go about with long threads of polyester filament clinging to my body. However, I had no idea that it would simply disintegrate in a quilt top when pressed with a hot iron.

Until now, I have been very casual about the use of thread. When people ask me what kind of thread I use for sewing my quilts, my usual reply has been, "Anything that matches." Now, I shall have to rethink my thread collection. I have nylon thread. From my embroidery floss, I strip out single threads to match my work. I keep boxes and boxes of 100-percent-cotton thread,

– – – –

some still on wooden spools. I have an enormous collection of cotton-covered polyester sewing threads on white plastic spools. I inherited old silk threads from dusty sewing boxes of my elderly aunts. There are metallic threads for special projects and a multicolored stash of quilting threads. These threads all have their places, but since seeing Jo's project, I think I had better sort them and use them only for the specific purposes for which they are intended.

I brought home some of Jo's peach-colored triangles and blue rectangles in various degrees of assembly, and I am helping her redo months of patient, precise work. Picking apart and resewing a large quilt is something that should never happen to anyone.

I sit here, and I am ripping. I am restitching. I am pressing. This quilt has a story to tell, and I am helping to piece it all together. This quilt has been to Oz, and like the Wicked Witch of the West, in a moment of excitement, it melted.

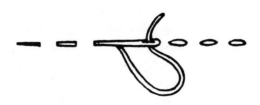

EENSY WEENSY SPIDER

LEGEND SAYS THAT ROBERT THE BRUCE, THAT GALLANT Scottish hero, rested in a cave on the Isle of Aran. He had lost six battles successively, and he was weary from war. The Bruce lay in that cave beside the sea, and he listened to the dashing waves outside, and he thought about his failures. He was tired and depressed. He may have heard the grunting of the seals on the shore, and he may have felt the damp mist as it drifted along the pebbly coast and climbed the hillsides thick with gorse and thistle. As he waited, resting, he looked up and saw, on the roof of the cave, a tiny spider swinging on its thread. Six times, the spider dangled and swung, trying to tack its filament across the mouth of the cave to anchor its web. Six times, it swung short and missed. On the seventh try, the little spider, who would not give up, caught the other side of the rock and went on to spin its fragile web. Every Scottish mother has told her child this story of how, after watching that persistent spider, Robert the Bruce went back into battle for the seventh time. That time he, too, won.

I have been working hard on a new quilt. It has gone together effortlessly, as smooth as warm butter. I found exactly the right fabric for each scrap, matched each color with ease. I cut each piece precisely and fitted the pieces together perfectly. Each block was straight and square. Making this quilt has been a joy from the word go. Everything went right . . . until now. Now I am put-

- - - -

ting the finishing touches on my quilt, seaming the blocks together into a wonderful medley. Every point is right, every thread is smooth, every edge even. Now that I am adding the final block, I cannot make it fit together. I have tried every trick I know, and I cannot make the seams meet accurately.

When I sewed the first side of this block in place and discovered that the points didn't meet, I took out the sewing machine stitches, turned the quilt top over, and stitched from the other side. They still did not meet. I took out the seam again.

I pinned the blocks together, putting pins exactly through the points on each side of the seam line, and I sewed it. I took it out.

Next, I put the pins a thread's width away from the seam line and sewed it. I took it out.

I pieced it in by hand. I took it out.

I laid the two right sides together and overcast the edges. The points should have met. I took it out.

I tried new thread, pins, light. I stood up, walked around my chair, sat down, picked up the block, and sewed it. I took it out.

I had a cup of coffee.

By this time, the edges of the blocks were tired and frayed. I pressed them and added some starch to give them back some life. I smoothed and pampered them. I spoke lovingly to them.

– – – –

This whole thing was getting to be more than I could handle. I was tempted to leave it sewn badly and hope that no one would notice. That little spider crept into my mind. It wrestled with its web, swinging back and forth, over and over. It did not give up.

I stiffened my jaw, picked up my own little thread, and I took a deep breath. With it, a fresh breeze came sifting through my mind, like the Scottish sea breeze blowing into the mouth of the cave. Like the spider, I tried one more time. I won my battle.

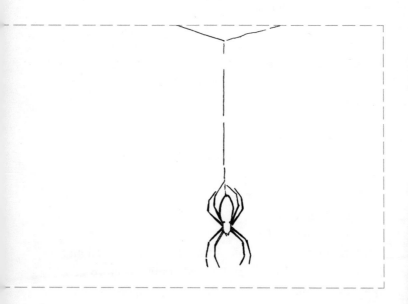

THE GREAT COVER-UP

WHEN MY SISTER NANCY WAS TINY, MY PARENTS TAUGHT her to recite the opening lines from the Punch and Judy shows. She would stand primly in her wee, short dress, with her hands clasped and an angelic expression on her face, and she would say, "Ladies and Gentlemen, how do you? If you'll be hippy, I'll be hippy, too."

"No, no," we would remonstrate. "Not 'hippy!' Say 'happy!'"

My sister would stamp her baby foot and howl, "I am saying 'hippy!' I am saying 'hippy!'"

Nancy and I have grown far beyond that cute stage of our long ago childhood. Now Nancy can pronounce the word "happy," and I have indeed become "hippy."

One of our favorite gifts that I make is a small, quick comforter, perfect for huddling under to watch TV in the evenings or for taking on a picnic to spread out on the pine needles for comfortable sitting. Sometimes I make these comforters in a simple pieced pattern out of the leftover fabric from my latest project. Sometimes I make them out of cheater cloth, or I use one of those printed panels of ducks and trees and mountains. I finish them with yarn ties for practicality and easy care. These quilts have multiplied over the years and have collected in piles in the corners of living rooms or in heaps on the ends of beds.

- - - -

When I first began giving these little comforters, I made them 45" x 60", the exact size of a crib quilt batt. Measuring or cutting the batt wasn't necessary. Eventually, I realized that two of my sons-in-law were well past the 6-foot measure and that all of my tall granddaughters were closing in on that. A 60"-long quilt was no longer adequate.

I began making the quilts 45" x 72" to cover those toe tips that stuck out when the quilts were pulled up to their chins.

Then last night, as I sat in the big recliner in the living room watching a PBS mystery, I began to realize that I felt decidedly cool, and I reached down to pull my own comforter around me to seal out the breezes. It was then that I had to face the fact that I now require more cover too, but I need it in the width of the quilt. Over the years, my body has progressed from no-hips to more-hips to hippy. Time plays tricks with the human body.

Over the centuries, quilts themselves have changed to fit a variety of bed sizes. Eighteenth-century families had enormous quilts that were meant to cover huge beds. In the mid-nineteenth century, quilts became smaller to fit three-quarter beds and narrow cot beds. My own bed is an old-fashioned double from the 1940s, a size nearly obsolete because people today prefer big queen- or king-sized beds. The covers for these beds

– – – –

are necessarily larger. I suppose it should be no surprise that my body measurements have changed with
the times, too.

Now, once more, I shall have to adjust my quilts. From
now on, when I make these little comforters, they will
be larger. Bigger is better. Bigger quilts will tuck around
bigger bodies, comfort restless souls, and seal out
evening drafts, and with these bigger quilts, I can be
both "hippy" and "happy."

MEASURE FOR MEASURE

THE MAILMAN RANG MY DOORBELL AND HANDED ME A padded envelope. What is more exciting than an unexpected package? The return address said Nebraska. It was a mysterious present from my daughter.

Inside I discovered a lovely piece of wood and a letter. She had found, she said, the answer to my dream.

We have always celebrated Christmas Eve at our house. We have hot Norwegian rice pudding baptized with brown sugar, melted butter, cinnamon, and juicy, rich red raspberries. All of the family comes, even those who live at a distance. Though we may go our own various ways the rest of the year, the evening of December 24th has, for all our lives, been sacrosanct, our own special family time.

To prepare for the evening, we carry the extra furniture out of the dining room. The deacon's bench is stored in the living room: the plant stands and side tables go into my workroom. We turn our old cherry dining table catty-corner and carry in a card table to extend it. Then, around the length, we put a variety of chairs, a stepstool for the littlest, a thick phone book to elevate the next smallest child, and so on.

This is not an ideal arrangement. Some guests must straddle table legs. The edges where the cherry table butts against the card table don't match. The card table is an inch lower, and it is narrower. The cloth that covers it lies in interesting convolutions. Dishes tend to slide into the crevasse.

One year we tried to put the children all together at the table in the back room. They felt left out, demoted. Another year we tried to divide the family, children and adults together, into two groups. Everybody felt left out. We have no other option than to pack everyone around our odd arrangement of tables and let them rub elbows and ankles with each other. As the number of grand-children increases and we include friends who plan to spend the evening alone, the problem compounds.

My dream, for years, has been to have a harvest table, the sort that is very long and narrow, but has two very wide drop leaves. When the leaves are opened, the table extends to a huge size, big enough to feed a fieldful of threshers.

I reasoned that I could drop the leaves and fit the very long, narrow table against the window wall for most of the year, but on the evening of the 24th, I would open it and cover it with a red and green quilt protected with a sheet of plastic. Upon this I would put my candles and evergreens and bowls of rice pudding. There would be ample room around the table for all the chairs, and the family would sit around it and laugh and love. My table would be a kind of family blessing.

I have searched through catalogs, visited furniture stores, talked to table manufacturers, and haunted an-tique stores for some years now. Nobody wants and nobody makes big harvest tables. Now, my daughter Faith had found a craftsman who would make me my table. In her package were the wood sample and the plans. The table would open to 8' x 8', and it would be finished with my favorite cherry stain.

I showed the drawings to a local furniture manufacturer. "Great plans," he said. "Go for it."

I have wanted this table for so many years, have been obsessed with the idea for it. It has been clearly etched on my brain, exactly what I wanted. Now that my dream is about to become a reality, common sense has taken over. I took two 4' measuring sticks from my workroom and laid them end to end across the dining room floor. Eight feet! I picked them up and laid them lengthwise to measure the other direction. For all the years I have had this dream in my head, I have never confronted it in a practical way. If I put an 8' table in that room, I will have two choices: either to knock out the walls or have the family stand up around it. There will be no room for chairs, no room to move into and out of the kitchen with dishes. The room is 12' square, which would leave 2' around on all sides.

I went around to my furniture manufacturer, and we talked common sense. "Do you realize," he said, "when you set a meal on that table for just the two of you, for just you and your husband, and you have the two big leaves dropped—do you know how far away from each other you will sit? Eight feet! That's how far!"

– – – –

I made excuses, like telling him that when just the two of us are home, we will eat at the back table. I am still clinging to my dream. I do not want to let it go. The dream of one night of the year with all the family sitting around one huge table in the candlelight is too beautiful to let go.

How could I have done this? I work with measurements daily. I am a quiltmaker, a needlewoman. I have an array of rulers and measuring tapes that would astonish a collector. Even without those, I am very accurate simply measuring with my eye.

I amaze my husband because I can look at a seam and say, "That's not ⌄". It's a ⅜" seam. It's ⅛" off." I can look at the center of a star and say, "That doesn't meet. It is a thread off. Take it out and do it again!" I can look at a hem and say, "That's 2∫ wide." I can hold a piece of fabric to my nose and stretch out my arm way back and know that I have measured a yard. You do it, too, don't you!

I arrive at many calculations with visual tools. To measure six feet, I mentally lay my husband down and figure from the soles of his feet to the tip of his head. I know how long 48" is because of those favorite measuring sticks, the ones I got at the bank giveaway and used to measure my dining room floor.

Eighteen inches is easy. It is the length of the hardware-store yardstick that I cut in half. I used the other half to prop up the window with a broken sash weight.

- - - -

One-fourth inch is the width of the seam I sew on my machine. These are easy measurements. I work with them every day.

So, where did I go wrong with my table measurements! I suppose it is because I am not used to working with eight-foot lengths. I should have known the size of my dining room. I know that I can put up a king-size quilt in a big frame in that room. The family has to crawl under it to get into the kitchen, and I have to sit very still while I work. Somehow, I didn't make any connection between a 120" X 120" quilt and an 8' table.

My husband can look at a car or a house, and he can tell you what is 10' or 15' or 20'. I have no idea how large our yard is. But his frame of reference is big sizes. He couldn't possibly see a ⅛", ¹⁄₁₆", or a ¹⁄₃₂" variation in a seam. Seams are not in his world, and 8' cherry tables are not in mine—only in my dreams.

I know there is a way I can have a big table if I am willing to alter my plan for size. The craftsman in Nebraska says he can make it any size I want, just not bigger than 8'. I have moved the furniture out of the dining room. I have stretched strings around it, measuring out different table sizes. It is all so abstract that I am frustrated. How can I make a considered decision? Years ago I made the decision to hang a door so that it would open in a certain direction. It was a bad decision, and I have had to live with it for years. How can I possibly make a decision on how big to make that table?

– – – –

If it were a quilt and the size were wrong (which it shouldn't be because I understand quilts), I could cut it off or add to it. But one cannot cut off or add to a table—and certainly not a cherry table with a lustrous finish.

I may have to put away my dream of a harvest table for want of a measure. Every now and then, I take my measuring sticks into the dining room and lay them out across the floor. I edge around them; I stand and stare at them. I do not even know how to begin to de-cide. Perhaps this December 24th, I will move all of the furniture out of that room and arrange chairs around the edges. Then, I will sit my family in the chairs and give them a quilt to stretch across between them. It will be something I can see, all of them in that room in their chairs with that quilt between them. Then, I can measure. Then I can understand because cause I understand quilts.

"M"

FOR SOME PEOPLE, "M" STANDS FOR MOTHER AND THE Many Things she taught them. At our house, "M" stands for May. That is, capital M, capital A, capital Y!

Our family has always loved celebrations. We have celebrated graduations, new babies, housewarmings, and sometimes we have been known to get together just to celebrate a lovely day.

Holidays have always been big with us. April Fool's is a time for shenanigans. Fourth of July requires us to go to parades, cook hamburgers over an open fire, watch fireworks, and slap mosquitoes. September is obligatory state-fair month. On Halloween, ever since the grandchildren could toddle, they have come to our house to dig into the costume basket. Some of those faded, tattered costumes belonged to their parents, and some even date from my own childhood, leftovers from dance recitals, school plays, and dress-up occasions. Octobers are months for pageantry. December holidays are filled with secrets and things hidden under beds.

Our May holiday is a truly wonderful one, our very own. Our family has birthdays scattered across the May page of the calendar. My own birthday in April bumps up against the end near early May. In May, my husband, two daughters, and a foreign-student daughter celebrate. Tantalizingly close in June come birthdays for a son-in-law and a granddaughter. May is the month for The Party.

– – – –

It's wonderful to have a whole month from which to choose a date. We can always find one day that suits everyone. Usually, if the weather is seasonably hot, we go to our daughter Jo's home and stand in her pool. Or maybe we will go to Muffin's where, when we open the windows, the cool, meadow-fresh air wafts in. Faith and her family usually drive up from Nebraska, and Connie completes the family roster.

If the weather is dreary, everyone comes here. Someone always brings buckets of fried chicken and coleslaw, and I usually go to the store and get a big cake that is decorated beautifully. I always check the half-price shelf first, and sometimes the cake will read, "Congratulations, Joannie," or "Happy Birthday, Tommy." I don't know who Joannie or Tommy are, but they didn't call for their cakes, and we get them marked down. We stick candles on them and sing and exchange gifts and laugh at the foolishness. Everyone always gets gifts, even the non-birthday people. It's our very own homemade holiday.

When they all come to my house, people sit everywhere—on chairs, on the couch, on stools, on the floor. The noise level soars. The energy bubbles. Usually there is considerable discussion about the quilt that I have in the frame.

One year, I impulsively gave one of my daughters a new small quilt from my stash. Now, one by one, I shall give each of the others one. I haven't told them out loud, but they all know. The suspense is heavy. I love suspense.

- - - -

The loveliest part of quilt giving is that they all treasure them. That first little birthday quilt that I gave hangs on my daughter's living-room wall, the shadowy wall away from the window. She treasures it. That's pretty exciting to give somebody a present that she wants so badly.

All of my daughters have quilted at one time or another. Each one sleeps under a quilt; each grandchild treasures his/her stack of little quilts piled on the foot of the bed; each husband has his own pieced comforter tucked behind a chair or onto the shelf of the front closet for late-night TV watching.

Now, as busy working women, my daughters find it more convenient to carry tiny counted-thread projects in their attaché cases. My granddaughters have kits with little cards of colored threads to sew. It pleases me that they, too, have made friends with the needle. They have learned the pleasures of turning basic, unadorned fabric into things of beauty. They have learned how to make their own rainbows and create their own seasons with their needles.

And because they sew, they can appreciate every stitch that I have taken. They know that I have spent early morning hours drafting and cutting and planning; late-night hours hunched under a lamp; bright daytime hours stitching; and long, long hours taking out and doing over—all because I had a dream in my head. When I give them my quilt, I am giving them my dream. That's nice, I think.

- - - -

The marvel of it is that there are so many quilters with these same dreams who are translating them into tangible visions to share. I am astonished by the numbers of people I see at quilt shows—the doers and the appreciators.

When I step out from the Quilt World into the Real World, it is astonishing for me to realize that this is really a special gift we have in quilting. In terms of the world population, we are a tiny portion of it. I am grateful that I can pass my dream along to my children.

It's May, lovely May, and I must sort through my quilts to see which daughter is to get the quilt surprise for this year's birthday. The excitement and suspense of it is almost more than I can stand.

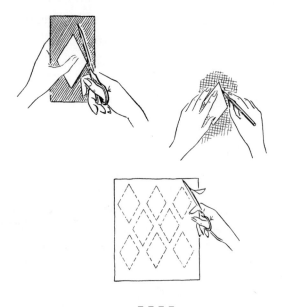

BYE BABY BUNTING

"MOM," SAID MY DAUGHTER ON THE PHONE LAST NIGHT. "Mom, you're going to be a grandmother again. What's the quilt going to be like?"

"Well, of course," said I, "this one will be a unicorn quilt."

Of the three Grandmother Quilts I have simmering on the back burner of my mind, that can be the only choice. This nearly new expectant mother is the one who, over the past years, has sent me pictures of unicorns. She has sent me statues and mobiles, little shining pieces of unicorns to hang in my window, magazine clippings, boxes, and assortments of other unicorn treasures. No doubt about it! This must be a unicorn quilt.

This news about being a grandmother again is not the sort that one deals with lightly just before going to bed. The effect is rather like eating a hamburger with onions or sticking a finger in a light socket. Last night I slipped into bed and pulled the quilt up under my chin. My whole body began to quiver. The wheels of my mind began to engage and grind faster and faster. My body flip-flopped. I forced myself to lie still. I folded my hands motionless on my chest, but my mind set up a filing system. It noted, collated, and indexed. It scheduled and sketched. All night long I mentally explored for and drafted pieced flowers. My head played

- - - -

with colors, finding marvelous combinations. It sorted through innumerable possibilities, exciting variations. I saw little unicorns and big unicorns, strutting unicorns, and reclining unicorns.

Whole new thoughts began to emerge, thoughts so exciting that I flip-flopped again. I tried to empty my mind. I told myself to lie flat, hands still. Toe, stop twitching! Say the alphabet backwards! Count to a thousand by sevens! I think I'll put a pomegranate tree on the quilt!

Now, it's six o'clock in the morning. Is it too early to get up and put on my fuzzy slippers and my bathrobe? The house is silent and chilly. The thermostat has not clicked on yet; the furnace has not begun to rumble. Will the family think I am insane if I slip downstairs and get out my quilt frame sawhorses and prop the old door across them to make my high worktable? Will I disturb them if I cut out a big piece of white paper and begin sketching and coloring?

I am up at last. I have come down, and I am sitting at the kitchen table inhaling the steam from my coffee cup. I am leafing through my books spread out around me on the floor, books with pictures and patterns and sketches. My mind is snapping and crackling. It is seven o'clock and the day is bursting with possibilities. I will be at the quilt shop by ten, waiting on the step for the shopkeeper to turn the key in the latch and open the door. I will buy wonderful fabrics in delicious colors. I

– – – –

will be home by noon to snip and cut and stitch. I will make a glorious picture for this new baby, and I will quilt it with tiny stitches. Others may paint cribs and knit booties, but I shall make a quilt and I must hurry. There's so little time, and so much to do!

THERE IS A SEASON

THE NEBRASKA FAMILY CAME UP TO VISIT. BILL AND I moved out of the big bedroom and set up a crib in the corner. I put a cot in my workroom for Bill and made up the extra bed in Connie's room for myself.

We had a wonderful week. All of the other children came home, too, and we crowded around the dining room table, straddling table legs. Grandchildren sat on step-stools and telephone directories. We drank gallons of milk and munched dozens of cookies. Little girls sat on the floor splashing color onto the pages of activity books, the washing machine ground out stacks of fresh clothing, the trash cans out back filled with used-up disposable diapers.

There was plenty of laughter, door-slamming, whispering, and telephone-ringing.

Today it is quiet. They have all gone—gone to their separate homes, gone back to their routines of daily living. The house has been put back in order. There are no boots in front of the door, no milk glasses in the sink, no apple cores in the wastebasket. Even the laundry basket is empty. So is my heart.

My husband and I sat and looked at each other. "I'm lonely," he said.

"So am I," said I.

"What'll I do?" he asked.

Well, I don't know what he's going to do, but I am

– – – –

going to make a quilt. I am going to begin it right now. I am going to get out my fabric and cover the floor with it. I am going to fill the room with the humming sound of my sewing machine, seasoned with a touch of good music and lovely sunshine coming through the window. I am going to feast on colors and textures. I am going to make my mind do gymnastics, my fingers fly. I'm going to make something soft and warm and wonderful.

I don't know what he's going to do, but I'm going to quilt.

- - - -

MY LUV IS NOT A RED, RED QUILT

I AM MAKING A RED QUILT, WELL, SORT OF. LET'S GO BACK to the beginning of this story. My granddaughter, Dani, got married. At the time of the wedding, I asked her if she would like a really nice quilted wall hanging for a gift. She looked wistful.

"What I would really like, Grandma," she said, "is a bed quilt."

"Oh...how big?" I asked.

"King-sized," she replied.

I had been thinking I could really throw myself into a nice, little wall hanging, say about 45" x 60". I was taken aback.

"Maybe I can make one that size for your twenty-fifth anniversary" I said. "At least I *hope* I get it finished before I live to be 102 and I die!"

For the next year, I made repeated calls and asked Dani to come by so that we could talk about pattern and colors. Time marched on. When I asked her mother about the delay, she told me that Dani was embarrassed because she didn't want to cause me a lot of trouble! From the moment Dani said, "King-sized," I knew that I was in trouble.

Finally, one night during a family dinner, I asked her point blank, "Dani, do you want a sweet, gentle quilt in soft blues and tans, or would you prefer a bright one in red and orange?"

– – – –

"Red, Grandma, really RED," she said without hesitation.

My local quilt shop advertised a sale. Three of my favorite words in all this world are "fifty percent off," so I went to the quilt sale. In the midst of the buying hysteria of the other quilters around me, I hauled bolts of red fabrics off the shelves and laid them out on the floor in a stunning array. The colors were definitely bold. They were gutsy. They sang to me. When one of the prints didn't quite fit into the progression of reds, I rifled through the untried fabrics and found one that suited quite well. Then I decided that it made another fabric down the line look a bit iffy.

I began shuffling reds like an excited child playing with her cards in a heated game of Old Maid. Finding the right-colored bolts is very hard work. While I perspired and sorted, shoppers took long steps across my fabrics laid out on the floor. Finally, carrying six bolts of glorious reds, I stood in the long, long line to have my fabrics cut and folded. I felt triumphant.

At home, I laid out my purchases on my workroom floor. They were wonderful, but they were not red. Stripped from the bolts in smaller pieces and folded smooth and flat so that they overlapped, the hues of red had turned rose. I rearranged them, but my quilt refused to look red.

Reaching back in my memory, I came up with something from my old Color Theory 101: "Use a complemen-

– – – –

tary color to intensify color." "Ah, ha!" I thought. "I need a good green to make my quilt look red-red." Back to the store I went and found a delicious green.

On my return, I laid my freshly cut green out with my reds. As I expected, the green was vibrant and stunning, but my rosy fabrics would not turn red.

This quilt that I am making is a flirtatious, demanding vixen. She tells me that she will not be red. Instead, she will be rose, a rich, shouting, vibrant rose. I've laid out my diamond pieces to form a great Lone Star, and I've filled the large squares and diamonds around the edges with pieced daylilies made with diamonds of the reddest of the fabrics. I've trimmed them with leaves made from the green. The flowers are spectacular, but they are not red. They are rose.

Dani has decided that she likes the rose-colored quilt, and so I must be content because these brilliant, shouting, vibrating colors make my heart happy. For the next year, I will be wallowing in this whale-sized quilt, stitching these fabrics together day after day, season after season, and I know now that it will not be a red, red quilt, because a rose is a rose is a rose.

BABY, TAKE A BOW!

I WENT TO A DANCE RECITAL LAST NIGHT. MY LITTLE GRAND-daughter stood on the edge of the stage in a white tutu. She wore a sequined crown and she clutched a sparkly, white, starry wand. Standing there wide-eyed and awed by the sea of faces beyond the footlights, she was elegant and awkward at the same time. She was innocent. She was wonderful. She was very young. The colors of her crown shot rainbows around her head. Would you like to see a picture of her? I carry some in my purse.

Last night was pure magic. My little girl had studied long and hard. In her trying, she had reached and stumbled. She had skinned her knee and bled a little. She had practiced and polished, and here she was at last, my little girl, a tiny ballerina. She stood frozen to the stage. She peered sideways to see what the next child was doing and then she began her elementary, childlike movements. She was Grace.

My first quiltmaking was like that, so long ago. I knew somehow that I wanted to make a quilt but I knew no other quilters. How did I begin in all my awkward newness? I read all that my library had to offer. There wasn't much back then. I clipped needlework articles from magazines and saved them in a big cardboard box. I experimented with techniques.

Then, I discovered a quilt kit in the bottom of a drawer in the upstairs guest room. The kit was so old that it must have been created in the Garden of Eden. It did

- - - -

indeed have flowers—purple tulips. It took me two years to appliqué those purple tulips with a tiny buttonhole stitch that I copied from a 1920s quilt. I pricked my fingers. I bled. I persisted. At the end of those two years, though, I had my first quilt. It was wonderful. Its tulips glowed like jewels. Hundreds of stitches covered the surface. It lay soft upon my bed. It was Grace.

Now I look at that quilt all these years later. The fresh glow has dimmed and I can see its awkwardness. I know that those hundreds of stitches are barely adequate. Like my granddaughter, I had to study another's performance to know how to do it. I stumbled many times, but when it was finished, that quilt had all of the potential of my little ballerina.

Someday she will molt her duckling feathers and emerge a dancing swan. Her movements will be flowing. She will make music with her body. Something similar, I hope, is happening to my quilts and to yours. I hope that every quilt we make will become more graceful, our movements disciplined. Our fingers will create swan music. The colors will glow. The sequins in our crown will turn to diamonds.

Tell me about your dreams for your quilts. What have you stitched lately? Is it glorious? I want to know about it, and I'll tell you about mine. Wait a minute—I have some pictures of it in my purse. If you have a moment, I'll show them to you.

- - - -

SITTING PRETTY

IT'S TIME TO MAKE A NEW FAMILY PICTURE. I USE THE word "make" advisedly. Let me tell you why.

When my friends have wanted to record their families on film, they have waited for all of the family members to gather for the big event. Then, scrubbed and polished, all of them have piled into cars and driven to a photographer's studio. In a few short moments, they are seated, snapped, and sent upon their way. Such a scheme would be an impossible scenario for our family. On those rare occasions when we are all gathered under a single roof, our get-togethers are loud and disorderly, which is not the ideal situation for taking pictures of angelically smiling children.

The last picture we "made" was at least six years ago. We can date it because my youngest grandchild is not in the picture, and there is not even a hint of his advent. We have changed a great deal since then. The toddlers in the picture are turning into young women now, and their parents are no longer twentyish.

I knew how to do the last picture because I am a quilter, and I did it the way I make a quilt. The man in the photography store said it couldn't be done. He said it would look obvious, amateurish. People later told us it must be great to get us all together as we were in the photograph. They had no idea that it was a pieced picture.

– – – –

This is how I will go about making our next family picture, too. First I will plan the design, just as with the last picture, and I will draft it exactly as I draft a quilt before I begin cutting and stitching. I will make this picture just as I would make a sampler quilt, with the same challenges of fitting all of the various colors and shapes together successfully. I have set out five chairs across one end of the living room. The middle chair will be the place for The Contrary Wife (that is I), and on one side I have designated a seat for The Prairie Queen and one for The Lady of the Lake. The other side is for my California Star and the Meadow Rose—all four daughters accounted for. Behind the chairs will stand the Cluster of Stars (the husbands), and kneeling in front will be the Ducks and Ducklings. See, just like a quilt! We will put the camera on the tripod and put it in a fixed position, focused directly on the chairs. No one is allowed to move it one inch. My tools are ready.

To make the first piece of our quilt, on a quiet evening when just Bill and I are at home, I will peel off my jogging/quilting suit and slip into a nice dress. Bill will put on a tie, and I will sit in my Wife chair. Bill will set the timer on the camera and race to stand behind me. We will smile perfect smiles, and the camera will flash. Each time one of the families comes to visit, we will sit the daughter in her chair and stand her Star behind her, and her Ducklings will kneel in front. They, too, will smile perfect smiles, and the camera will flash.

- - - -

When I have put together my Ladies and their Stars and their flocks of Ducklings, I will be ready to set my quilt picture together.

I will go to the photography shop and have each of the single-family pictures printed. Then, with the craft knife I use for cutting stencils, I will, oh so carefully, cut out each set of people and fit them into the scene with the same wall, the same door, the same desk behind. The man in the photography shop said the cut edges would be obvious. I cut carefully, beveling slightly under the edges and touching any telltales with the tiny tip of my permanent marker, the one I use to sign my quilts.

When I have pieced my quilt and put it together, I need to finish it properly, so I will take my creation to the photographer to take a picture of the picture. Voila! When I made the first picture quilt. the photography-store man was astounded. I wasn't. I have been putting scraps of fabric together for a long time. I didn't doubt that I could do it with photos, too.

Now it's time to start the second paper family reunion quilt. We have a new Star for this one and a couple more Ducklings that need to be pieced in. It just gets better and better.

PLYING MY TRADE

WE ALL WENT OUT FOR DINNER—MY HUSBAND BILL, my daughter Connie, my brother, and me. We went over to a little store-front Vietnamese restaurant that's not far from our house, but since the weather had turned cold and icy, it only made sense to drive the car. Bill, of course, was up front, with Connie beside him. My brother was in back with me. I sat behind Bill.

Not far from the restaurant, Bill stopped the car in front of a driveway so that Connie and my brother could get out easily without hurdling a curb. I hopped out on my side and scurried around behind the car. As I came to the driveway apron, my foot hit the incline of the curb, and I skidded. I grabbed hold of the door handle, slipped a bit, and down I went. Now, if you live in some wonderful place like Florida or Arizona or California, you may not relate to what happened. If you live in the cold north, however, you know that whenever you slip next to a car, whether it is magnetism or gravity or whatever, you almost always fall beneath that car.

Connie said, "Don't back up, Dad. Mom is lying in the street under the car."

My brother said he saw a moment of hesitation, a flicker of temptation flash across my husband's face, but charity won out. He paused only a moment with his foot between the accelerator and the brake. His foot tromped on the brake.

I lay there in the snow that wasn't very cold, and I laughed at the absurdity of the situation. I wasn't even embarrassed, because there wasn't anybody to see my clumsiness except those nearest and dearest to me, and they know me so well.

Connie and my brother slipped and slithered trying to get a foothold so that they could haul me to my feet. They each took hold of an arm and pulled, and then I was up, and Bill parked the car. I brushed off the snow, we all laughed, and that was the end of that, I thought.

A week later I still had a kink in my hip. It didn't even hurt really. It just made me go up and down the stairs in a sort of crablike fashion, and even that stiffness wore off shortly.

Now, here I am working to finish my quilt. I have my favorite chair pulled up to my frame in my sunny back room. There are my two good lamps, one at the top of the frame, and one over my left shoulder. I have my pincushion and my snippers and thread heaped in the center of the quilt and my pliers. God bless those pliers! I didn't know I had wracked my thumb in that fall. It didn't hurt then and it doesn't hurt now except for a sort of little catch in the heel of my hand when I twist it a certain way. I just can't get hold of the needle. I can push it into the layers of fabric, but I cannot yank it through. Now, doesn't that beat all! Quilting here in the sunshine,

– – – –

pushing the needle, grabbing it, and tugging it with the pliers gives me time to think things out.

What if my thumb is permanently klutzed? I am not panicked because it is obvious that I have worked out a way to handle the situation. But I am in the same predicament that I have watched so many other quilters work through. Suddenly, I have to change my work pattern. I have dealt with changing eyesight by simply getting stronger glasses and brighter lights, but what are some of the possibilities for dealing with a limp thumb?

Now I can appreciate those quilters who have perfected ways to machine quilt. I love to hand quilt, and I truly think that perhaps it is the happiest thing that I do, sitting, listening to music while my hand dips and my quilt fluffs. Maybe I will have to take my pleasure some other way. I can ask other quilters to finish my quilts, but I love the puzzle of figuring out from moment to moment how to make my quilt top come to life and to say what I mean it to say—the spontaneity of quilting a line to see if it does what I hope it will—and trying another and another way.

I have tried using a bigger needle. My thumb won't grasp the end of a #10, but I found that I can take hold of a larger needle tip. And what's more, my stitches aren't much bigger. Oh, joy of joys.

It would have been easier if I hadn't used hard polished cotton fabric in this quilt. Quilting it is like puncturing oilcloth. Doing this quilt is more difficult, too,

– – – –

because I tend to quilt the bejeebers out of things, and to quilt across difficult areas like where eight points come together. Perhaps I will need to find simpler patterns and easier routes across my quilts.

I am a positive thinker—I really believe that my foolish thumb will get better and the aggravation will go away. Certainly the exercise of quilting should improve it. Though I was gloomy about the whole situation this morning, I know now that even with a temperamental thumb I can go on doing some kind of quilting. It may not be wonderful work and it may not be in the style I have been used to all these years, but even with a "dumb thumb" I can go on sitting here in the sunshine, quilting, working a bit more slowly, a bit differently; but I can do it. I remember what my mother used to say: "If at first you don't succeed, ply and ply again."

CHAPTER 6
A Stitch in Time

FACING THE NEW YEAR

JANUS WAS THE ROMAN GOD OF GATES AND LOCKS, and his powers had to do with "comings and goings." His temple in Rome was aligned with the directions of the sunrise and the sunset, and he was usually pictured with two faces, one old, one young, looking in opposite directions. The old one must have grown that way from remembering past indiscretions and stumblings. The young face must have represented the universal naiveté of believing that one will not be indiscreet or stumble. January was named for this god who looks back and looks forward at the same time.

January is a good time to take stock. After the miasma of December holiday preparations, the celebrating and the recovery, the first thing I do is to make an appointment for a physical, followed by a dental exam and an eye test. I call the garage and schedule an oil change for my car. With my parts and my equipment in good working order, I clean the refrigerator, scrubbing the spilled orange juice from under the vegetable bin. The first of January is a time to pause and refresh during that perfect interval between the pressures of the holidays and winter activities.

I was ready for January. My sewing machine was threaded and waiting for me. A vision of my next quilt played through my head when I went to bed at night. I delayed buying fabrics until I had the time to think seri-

– – – –

ously about this project. With my work table in good order and no more necessary chores left for me to do, I was ready for the inventing of this new quilt.

I had my tools set out, and I turned on my sewing machine. I pressed the foot control, and the machine made a chirping noise. This is not right! My machine should whir; it should not chirp!

Using my miniature screwdriver, I removed the throat plate, and I flicked at the feed dogs with my tiny brush, whisking away the lint. I released the bobbin case and put a drop of oil on the bobbin race. I reassembled my machine. It chirped again.

I have been conscientious about maintaining my body, my car, my home, and even my laundry equipment, but I neglected the health of my sewing machine. Now my best friend, my consoler, my companion, is ill. When I called the sewing machine store, the repairman said that if I leave my machine with them, they will phone me when they have completed their diagnosis and pampered it until it purrs like a healthy, contented kitten. This means, of course, that my machine and I must be separated.

In December, I made gifts of glowing soft colors, neatly pieced and carefully quilted. I look back on that time with satisfaction. My machine worked hard for me, but it has become achy and arthritic. The older face of Janus sighs with sympathy for my weary machine. When

I surrender it to the repairman, I will play with the visions in my head. I will make quilt sketches. I will shop for fabric and wash and iron the material so that I will be ready when my machine comes home to me, rejuvenated and filled with enthusiasm. Then young Janus will smile his bright smile, for it is January and together my machine and I shall explore all of the exciting possibilities and tempting adventures of this new year.

STORMY WEATHER

WHEN I WOKE THIS MORNING, I COULD HEAR THE WIND muttering. The snow drifted down in large, spongy flakes, filling the crotches of the trees and making little frosty bundles on the tops of the evergreen branches. As I ate my breakfast, the temperature warmed just a tad. The snow turned wet. It stuck to the sidewalks and gutters and tops of cars, then hardened, and turned to slick ice, coating everything it touched. Still the snow came down. The light was dim and gray.

Why does grim weather make me restless? I turned on all the lights in my workroom to make it cheerful and inviting, made a full pot of hot, fragrant coffee, and had rollicking music ringing from my little radio, but I still felt edgy and bedraggled. I began to cut pieces for my new quilt. The colors irritated me; they seemed wrong. I thought I had planned it carefully. I pulled materials from my cupboards and made piles on the floor, and then draped them in color groupings. My choices had seemed right at the time. This morning the fabrics were too bright, too dull, too blue, too rose. They did not make me happy, and so off I went to the quilt store.

So did everybody else. I was at the store soon after the shop owner unlocked her doors and welcomed the avalanche of quilters. I wedged in among them. We chatted. We fingered fabric. We told each other stories about our homes and our quilts. We took the bolts off the shelves and spread all of that delicious fabric across every horizontal surface.

– – – –

We laughed, fingered it some more, and then we bought. Being in that room with all those quilters was a sort of communion. There was comfort and consolation in the sharing.

Life would be quite satisfactory if the weather were glorious, and flowers were springing up around me. I would be enormously cheerful to be stitching while sipping fresh pressed cider and listening to the sounds of me neighbors gathering for family picnics. I would be happy to be out walking a path across the hills through rustling leaves. But this weather was not satisfactory, cheerful, or happy. It was decidedly bleak.

To get to the quilt shop on this dismal morning, I had to scrape the ice off the windshield of my car, back the car out into the driving, blinding snow, and creep four miles along frozen streets. Coming in from all that dreariness into the brightly lit quilt shop made the colors radiate more wonderfully. It made our designs seem grander, and made the quilters generous and supportive. A quilt shop is the panacea for a dreary day.

I am home now, and I am cutting the fabrics that I just bought. The colors are vivid and compelling. They blend cleverly; they are perfect! They speak to the of laughter and of friendships on this murky, cheerless day, and as I shape my quilt, I smile.

I hum an old, jazzy blues tune as I snip out my patchwork pieces. "Don't know why, there's no sun up in the sky," I sing. The weather storms outside my windows, but suddenly, inside I have that old sun in my sky.

– – – –

AM I BLUE?

AT THIS VERY MOMENT, I AM QUILTING ON A DARK BLUE quilt. Well, maybe not at this exact moment. At this exact moment, I am talking to you. I've put down my needle, and I am leaning on the rail of my quilt frame and I am gasping for breath. So, at this exact moment, I am talking to you about how I feel about this dark blue quilt.

When I was a small child, I had a complete wardrobe of blue. I had blue dresses with blue bloomers. A blue coat. Blue nighties. Everything I wore was blue. My mother thought that I looked adorable in blue with my clear blue eyes, my hair bleached blond by the southern sun, and my freckles darting across my nose.

Actually, I was too young to worry about whether I looked darling or not, but I thought blue was pretty nice. When I was a little older, old enough to read, my favorite poem (which I still recite when prompted) was an A. A. Milne poem about Nanny's blue dressing gown. At that time, Shirley Temple was my alter ego in her technicolor screen version of "The Blue Bird." By the time I got to high school, I wrote a truly terrible poem called, "Blue's My Favorite Color."

Some time after this, I discovered that the world is made up of other colors, reds and yellows and purples. I fell in love with the spectrum and painted my living room green and bought peach-colored dresses. Aside from dashing to the window when a blue jay flashed by

– – – –

my window in mid-winter, blue took a definite back seat in my life.

When I began quilting, occasional sparks of blue danced in my quilts—aquas, sky blues, gentle powdery blues, or exciting electric hues. Several years ago, I took on the challenge of making for a friend a quilt that would set off a piece of indigo blue given to her as a wedding gift. This deep. dark blue was a whole new experience for me. It was an African tie-dye and had fish and swirls across its surface. I rinsed out the excess dye and set it with broad borders to make a queen-sized quilt. At the beginning of March that year, I set up my largest quilt frame and began to stitch. I stitched from morning to evening and far into each night. I surrounded myself with 100-watt lamps to ward off the March gloom, and I stitched and stitched. By the end of March I felt 100 years older. I knew that I should have never taken on a queen-sized indigo quilt in dreary light. It does not take very much intelligence to see that 12,240 square inches of indigo blue quilting does not encourage good mental health in the depths of March gloom.

When the quilt was finally done, I vowed that it was my last dark blue quilt. I have a short memory.

When I began the quilt that I am working on now, it was April. The grass was turning green. The tulips were emerging, the birds singing. I splattered raspberry-colored pieces across the quilt and sparkled it with hun-

– – – –

dreds of tiny white beads. It was a joyful quilt, even if it did have six different shades of dark blue.

April has passed—and May. The sky is a sweet, gentle blue. The irises in the garden are rich, enthusiastic blues. Next door, my neighbor's blue plastic sunflowers are whirling in the wind, and here am I struggling to tug my needle through six shades of dark blue fabric. I chose the main fabric because it is so dense, the batting cannot possibly beard through it. Now I find that the fabric is so tough, I need pliers to pull my needle through it.

This month is not March, but like the making of that March quilt, I wonder if I will survive this one. Each stitch gets harder, each moment longer. Look here. I've reached the end of this row. Let me turn the quilt in the frame. And now—do I dare believe?—only six inches more of quilting and I will be done! Oh, the joy. If I make myself a cup of coffee and if I really work hard, it'll be done by supper, all quilted with its raspberry pieces and sparkling beads. I'll thread my needle and run it along this line and the fabric will swell up in these final loops and it will look wonderful. I'll just slip my needle in here and snap the thread knot inside, and tug it through.

And suddenly the music changes. The slow, forever beat of the dirge swings into a red-hot version—a sassy, snappy version—of my old Mood Indigo.

— — — —

A CURE FOR A COMMON COLD

SPRING COMES LATE HERE. BY THE END OF FEBRUARY, we find ourselves raging at the interminable snow. Nature teases us by granting us an occasional thaw, just warm enough to lay bare the lawns, and then she sifts more snow across the landscape. Old-timers, like ancient midwives, tell horror stories, recounting the years that snow has come as late as May, covering the brave daffodil blooms with a heavy, wet shroud. Storytellers lick their lips, telling and retelling these stories, defeating our hope that spring will ever come.

These days I have two ways of buoying my spirits, of fighting back the prospect of eternal snow. First, I indulge myself in the ancient art of chunk kicking. This is a late-winter ritual that I was taught early after my arrival in this land of whiteness. The game may not be unique to Minnesota, but I was taught it here, and so I cherish it as a peculiarity of this area. Chunk kicking is merely this: throughout winter an accumulation of sand and salt builds up on the roads. It creates a grimy, slushy snow that spews off the backs of whirling car wheels, builds up between the tires and the fenders, and creates ugly, dirty deposits of ice chunks. With every foray to the grocery store, new chunks develop, each grimier than the last. The therapeutic effect of swinging a vicious kick to the filthy lump, knocking it loose and sending it sprawling, is

– – – –

inexpressible. Joy surges through your body. The elation becomes heady. I find myself wandering through parking lots kicking other people's chunks, thrashing out at winter.

The second thing that I do in a prolonged winter is to make flower quilts. Looking through my album of quilt pictures, I realize that my flower quilts are, for the most part, late winter ones. One quilt is covered with tulips, and one has roses and shamrocks. One has strips of irises and lilacs, and another is trimmed with bleeding hearts and morning glories.

Just seven days ago, we had a glorious week when the snow melted and the thawing ice ran down the center of our alley in a real gully washer. The lawn poked through its winter cover and little sprouts appeared in the garden. The sun shone in a warm, benevolent glow. Then, it snowed! If we run out of milk at a time like this, we must go out and stomp through the snow to warm the car. We most surely will slip on the ice and fall. It will be wet. It will be cold. Inside, in my comfortable workroom, there is an assortment of flower drawings with little piles of brightly colored scraps laid out on the floor. This spring's flower quilt is in process. Making a quilt takes just long enough that, when the last stitch is sewn, spring will really have come.

Even though spring does come every year, it is always later than we could wish it. To get a good start on it, some people plant hope. They set out peat pots sown with seeds. They put up special lights for them, water them, and wait impatiently for them to sprout into embryo plants, delicate feelers of faith reaching up to them in this chilly season. I plant my own flowers in fabrics. and I get instant blooms, glowing and soft to the touch. I fill my workroom with these flowers, bathe them in the glory of my 100-watt sun, sprinkle them with love and attention, and create my own perfect springtime.

Indeed, spring comes late here, and I have two ways of fighting the late winter grime and snow. I chunk kick, and I sow flowers. Flowers are better.

GRANDMOTHER'S FLOWER GARDEN, KINDA

WOULD YOU BELIEVE I HAVE JUST FINISHED MAKING a Grandmother's Flower Garden quilt? It has changed my outlook on quilting. Let me tell you about it.

I was in a little variety store, the old-fashioned kind with little nooks and crannies and uneven floors. I love to look at the unusual flat-fold fabrics in stores like that, to discover the whimsical, strange, and sometimes weird patterns that you can turn over in the piles and piles of material that are folded in lengths and stacked on bargain tables. While I was digging through a great pile of fabric of dubious fibers, I came across a short length of cloth that made me rock back on my heels and take a second look. I burst out laughing. Hexagons spiraled in the air like spots before my eyes. I seized upon that fabric and went straight to the cutting table. The fabric measured two yards minus two inches, not quite two. "Well," said the clerk, "I think we should call this a yard and two-thirds." I gleefully carried away my treasure in a brown paper sack.

All that day, I carried that sack with me. I fingered it lovingly and every now and then I pulled the fabric out of the bag to study it and laugh some more. There were faces all over it, a strange assortment of faces: poets, actors, and politicians from times and places that had no relationship except that each was drawn in gray lines on a piece of cotton-poly blend.

– – – –

I counted faces. Yes, just as I had hoped, there were enough faces that I could make 23 flowers in a Flower Garden if I made two William Shakespeare dahlias and filled in the odd corners with Katharine Hepburn. I couldn't wait to get home and start cutting out hexagons.

Let me say here, that I have always been rather smug and patronizing about Grandmother's Flower Gardens. I have called them The All-American Quilt. I have seen dozens of them, maybe hundreds, maybe thousands. Some of them have been finished masterpieces, many less artfully done, but by and large the majority of them have been rumply, undisciplined, undistinguished quilt tops folded away in drawers or tucked onto closet shelves. The quilt that I was planning was to be the funniest, sassiest Flower Garden ever. Thus began my odyssey into my field of flowers.

I got out my *Quilter's Newsletter Magazine* Index and looked up "Grandmother's Flower Gardens." Then, digging into my stack of magazines, I laid out all of the issues that included hexagons on my floor, gardens looking up at me. I studied them. I thought to myself, "Well, when you've seen one you've seen 'em all."

I didn't have a wide choice of design if I wanted to be traditional. There were a few pink paths among the gardens I studied, but green seemed to be the overwhelming choice. There was a center hexagon, often yellow, but not always. This was surrounded by six bright, solid, flower-colored hexagons. Next, there was a ring of printed hexagons, and then a ring of white or pale pastel ones to set off the flower. These were laced together with pathways. A simple formula.

I did notice that there seemed to be all sorts of ways the quilts were finished. Sometimes the edges were neatly turned in on themselves to form a jaggedy shape around the outside of the quilt. Sometimes the points were chopped off, sometimes filled in, sometimes appliquéd on a solid strip or bound off to make an even edge. Sometimes the quilts were simply unfinished with the batting and threads still dangling from the raw edges. I would find out why later.

I studied the pictures on my fabric and made a series of six-sided holes in a piece of paper to determine what size hexagon would frame my faces best. When I had studied Flower Gardens in the past, I had been charmed by a particular quilt that was made of tiny hexagons and had little green triangles inset in patterns along the paths. My fabric faces were too large for "itty bitty" hexagons. I drew a 2" circle, drafted a hexagon from it, and it was exactly right. Using this for my pattern, I began to cut scrap paper into perfect hexagons.

I had decided to paper-piece with the English method because I had seen an astonishing number of hand-pieced Flower Garden quilts that had little tucks sewn into them, or were wavy and soft and totally unmanageable. Surely, English paper piecing would make a smooth, flat, perfect quilt top, and the tiny bit of English blood that flows through my veins qualifies me for the stamina and determination required to do this style of patchwork.

Using my pattern, I cut out paper hexagons. I cut out paper hexagons and I cut out paper hexagons and I cut out more paper hexagons. I had a cup of coffee and cut out some more. I went to bed for the night and got up in the morning and cut out more. I took to counting my paper hexagons. I had no desire to cut out one single hexagon more than I needed. I cut out more hexagons and soon had a shoe box filled. It was time to cut out fabric hexagons!

Fabric hexagons would surely go more quickly. I could cut them with my small rotary cutter and since my paper hexagons were perfect, a little variation in the fabric pieces was tolerable. I cut out fabric hexagons.

I began to accumulate sandwich bags filled with bright colored pieces. I cut out more hexagons. I cut out more hexagons. I filed them in shoe boxes. I cut out more hexagons.

One rosy morning, I laid out all my pieces on the living room rug. I had enough to begin my quilt top! They looked wonderful. I chortled. This was going to be just fine.

I made a nest for myself on the couch. I propped pillows around me and arranged my spools of thread and pins on the end table. There were shoe boxes and sandwich bags placed around me in a ring. My scissors and pincushion were within reach. Like an old settler

– – – –

ready for a long winter, my provisions were put in, and I was ready.

I pinned one hexagon face onto a hexagon paper, folded the fabric edges over it, and basted around to hold them in place. I basted another one. It was fun to see my fabric turning into patchwork pieces. I basted more, stacked them, and ran a thread through them to tie them together. Heaven protect me from losing even one! I basted more, and basted and basted.

I came to understand in all that basting that the reason our mothers made Flower Gardens was that they were a *tour de force.* Just as every new quiltmaker in the 1970s wanted to make a Lone Star Quilt, surely the dream of every new quiltmaker in the 1920s and '30s was to make a Flower Garden.

I began laying out my hexagons, little centers, colored rings, and then the rings of little faces echoing round and round looking back and laughing at me. I basted more hexagons.

As the evenings wore on, I began to pin the hexagons together, face to face, and overcast the seams. The flowers actually took shape in my hands. The going was slow but I was watching the sprouts begin to bloom and it was exciting.

The repeating shapes talked to me, explained the fun our mothers had when they stitched in those scraps with little nursery-rhyme characters, tiny sailboats, farm animals.

I became obsessive. My husband asked me if I ever

went to bed. When he turned in at night, I was sitting on the couch making flowers. When he got up in the morning, I was sitting on the couch making flowers.

I discovered something new about paper piecing. Clutching all of that paper-filled fabric, my hands began to stiffen. Hot dishwater helped. I found myself rubbing my knuckles. I was driven. I overcast more hexagons together. Then came the day that I laid out 23 flowers on my living room floor, 23 flowers all flat and even and perfect. Twenty-three sets of faces swirling round and round! Now to put them together among their green pathways!

I will admit that rolling up all of those papery flowers to pin and shape and stitch them was akin to crumpling up a phone book in my hands. I was not prepared for the bulk of what I had created, but when you have doggedly pursued a Flower Garden this far, you do not throw down your hoe! The end was in sight. I clutched! I stitched! And one lovely day, I spread out my garden—flat, smooth, and with flowers blooming. There were no weeds, no mites. My garden was perfect. I snipped my basting threads and then removed papers gleefully. I had triumphed. I had made a Garden...

I prepared for quilting. I wouldn't wait. I stretched out my backing, bigger than I needed so that it would fit comfortably into the frame. I was thinking ahead, you see. I thought I was thinking of everything. I basted down the jagged edges running along the sides. I

– – – –

basted heavily. Oh, this was going to be great! Just great! What was a little basting compared to those days of cutting and stitching hexagons?

I set out my frame and dropped my quilt into it. Everything I needed was at hand: good light, lots of needles, some radio music, coffee. Life was lovely. The traditional way of quilting a Flower Garden is simple double-outline quilting, one-quarter inch each side of every line. Because I love quilting, and because I went at it with such exhilaration, I was halfway through before I realized that instead of quilting my hexagons in sets of three, if I turned my frame sidewards, I could quilt across in straight lines of hexagons and work twice as fast. Oh, well, only a little time lost! I speeded up my breakneck pace. I quilted the middle. I quilted down the middle to the straight edges on the end. I quilted a little to the sides of the middle. Like Scarlett O'Hara, I saw a big problem ahead of me, but I was skirting the issue. I would worry about it tomorrow.

What I saw looming ahead of me was the question of how to quilt those uneven edges. If I quilted right to the edge, how would I be able to turn them in on each other? If I didn't, but left them free, how could I possibly control them to get them to fall exactly in place to quilt AFTER I had overcast the edges? Aha! Now I understood all of those quilts that have the edges whacked off or they are filled in or bound off or appliqued down. I faced a dandy challenge.

– – – –

In the end, after much agonizing, I went ahead and quilted the outer edges first. I held the loose edges in place and quilted them down. Then, taking the quilt out of the frame, I trimmed off the excess backing, leaving only the quarter-inch seam allowance, and with a big darning needle, tucked in the seam allowance edges and overcast them. It was not easy, not easy at all.

I finished my Flower Garden this morning. I am pleased with it. I have a new, true appreciation of the old masterpiece Flower Gardens, the ones that got finished so beautifully. Now that I have done IT, I will never be flippant about Flower Garden quilts again. I understand and sympathize with all of the unfinished ones. I applaud the complete ones. I love mine.

My husband came and stood beside me. He looked at my quilt as it was laid out, finished, on the floor.

"Hey," he said. "It's great. You know what you can do next? *The Wall Street Journal* has faces exactly that size. You could make a quilt and call it, 'A Meeting in the Rose Garden.' On one flower you could have Republicans and Democrats. On another you could have big businessmen and environmentalists. You could bring together all of the world's adversaries, all of the quarreling and disputing people of the world in a rose garden."

He's right. It's a great idea. But one Flower Garden is enough. Somebody else should make a Rose Garden quilt though, and please, if it is you, send me a picture of it so that I can love it too.

– – – –

HOW DOES YOUR GARDEN GROW?

THIS YEAR I AM GIVING MYSELF JULY. I HAVE BEEN OUT pruning the roses. They were burdened with deadwood and mildew from years of neglect. I do not understand how they have survived. Just pure stubbornness, I guess! I have a few thorns and blisters in my quilting hands, but nothing I can't manage. Always before in July I have been busy, too busy to putter, to dream, to savor. This year, July is mine.

During the second week of May every year, I am seized with springtime frenzy. The trees are leafing out by then. The world is a mixture of aqua blue and a soft, new green against the sky. The birds have come back. The ground is warm. And when I see my first dandelion, I lose my senses. I abandon my quilt frame. During the long winter I have treated my hands with respect. I have protected my calloused right middle finger. I have encouraged the hard, pricked surface on my second finger, left hand. I have tended my hands with all of the quilters' cures and devices: healing detergent water, alum, New Skin, lotions, thimbles, and Band-Aids. But suddenly it is the second week in May, and my annual craziness comes over me. I abandon myself to the warm earth. I grub in the dirt with my bare hands. I pull weeds. I sprinkle seeds.

I have a theory about gardens: If I weed thoroughly and plant seeds thickly, the new plants will grow dense. The leaves will intertwine over the garden, and any weed that is spunky enough to grow underneath will never be

– – – –

seen. The zinnias and cosmos will burst into an explosion of color above it all.

Only, ordinarily I never see the flowers when they burst into bloom in July. By then, I have cleaned my nails and removed the splinters. I am back at my rushing around, being too busy to enjoy all that beauty.

As a quilter, I find this rather shocking. Quilters always treasure their gardens. Otherwise, why would the Flower Garden Quilt have been the number one favorite of our grandmothers? Why would we have so many lily patterns, the peony, the dahlia, the tulip? Why all those wonderful roses, the queen of gardens and quilt collections? Flowers in gardens and quilts are to be treasured.

This year July is mine. I shall quilt. In my contentment, I shall watch my garden bloom. Perhaps I shall quilt something with flowers. If I do, it will be in hazy colors like those of the early morning when the grass is still wet and my flowers glint a bit here and there. I think it should be in soft oranges, reds, and golds like my zinnias. It must, too, have some of the boldness of nasturtiums and coreopsis. July is a time for gardens and quilts. This year July is mine.

– – – –

AS YE SOW, SO SHALL YE SEW

IT'S TIME TO START THINKING ABOUT WHAT TO PLANT in the garden. The seed packet racks are beginning to appear in the grocery stores and the vegetable and flower catalogs are filling the mail slot.

Our garden has dwindled from a large plot behind my in-laws' house to a couple of plants in the back yard, but my husband, Bill, does wonderful things with whatever he decides to put in. He comes from a long line of gardeners who figure that bigger is better, and one year he grew a rutabaga that put up leaves so large and glossy it looked like a bush. I have a picture I took of him when he finally dug up the rutabaga, all purple and yellow and hairy. He was grinning gleefully. He was enormously proud of that rutabaga, even though it was so tough and thready that we couldn't eat it.

I made him a quilted wall hanging that I called "Rutabaga Rex." This heraldic banner features fierce rabbits and dandelions and even one small caterpillar. It grew tiresome explaining to people that all that gold fringe and the tassels and opulent bunting was purposely gaudy, and so, rather than bring it out anymore, I fastened the quilt to the wall over our bed. Now, we sleep beneath it in baronial splendor.

One year Bill decided to make his own seed tape. He unrolled a length of toilet paper, ran a bead of white glue down the center and embedded the seeds. Once it was planted, the tissue degraded almost instantly, but the seeds were entombed in the glue for eternity. Not a single one ever sprouted.

Another year, he poked at the pile of dirt that covered the pit where he had been burying the dog messes for a year and announced that it had composted adequately. One of my daughters shoved a single sunflower seed into that dirt. The sunflower plant grew so tall that we took a picture of her standing on a step ladder beside it. In the end, she dragged the entire plant, flower and all, a half mile to school for Show and Tell. She remembers to this day thinking there was never anything so heavy in all the world.

The best planting experience was the year that Bill delayed putting in our annual two tomato plants. When he finally bought them and set them out, they didn't produce fruit until frost time. He is not one to give in to Old Man Winter, so he carried out a clear, plastic table cloth and made a tent around the plants. Then he dragged out a heavy-duty electrical extension cord and an old hair dryer. The hair dryer droned away under the tent in the back yard all fall. We had delicious vine-ripened tomatoes until Thanksgiving. By mid December, the tomatoes began to taste strangely, sort of greenish and moldy. When we inspected them, we found tiny, white, stringy things inside. Those stringy, white things were seeds sprouting. We turned off the hairdryer, took down the tent and conceded to the ice and snow.

– – – –

Bill makes gardens like you and I make quilts. Going to the quilt store is, for us, like when he studies seed catalogs. We see fabrics that send our imaginations into fits of fancy. I saw a glorious scrap yesterday, rich black with red paisley swirls. It was beguiling. At guild meetings, you and I are intrigued with all of the new, lovely quilts. They make our minds gyrate and our fingers itch. When we pick up a book and see something new, a quilt, a tree, a flower, a sunset, or when we look out of our windows, we have visions. Something happens in our heads and our hearts. A seed is planted, so that when we make our quilts there is a piece of us that is stitched into them. We nurture that first inspiration. It ripens and blooms.

Have you noticed that when you try to describe to people what your quilt vision is, their eyes glaze over? They can't see into your mind. Your dream is so personal that you need to make that quilt so you can watch your vision grow. Quiltmaking is a passion and a compulsion that is a gift to us, like planting those seeds is for a gardener. The vision may be beautiful, it may be funny, it may be sad. It may be all of those things. The possibilities are as tantalizing as the seed packets with golden, fleshy squash or dazzling zinnias printed on the front. The lucky thing about quilts is that we can plant them in any season, and they will bloom.

RECONSIDERING THE LILIES

WHEN I GOT BACK FROM THE GROCERY STORE THIS AFTER-
noon, my husband Bill wasn't anywhere to be found in
the house. That being the case, I went straight out to
look for him. Bill borrowed one of those high pressure
water hoses to wash the flaking paint off the side of our
house. He is gearing up to give the house a face lift, and
he hopes to avoid all the scraping and sanding that usually accompany the preparation for painting.

Bill was warned that one of three things could happen with the hose contraption: he could blast a hole in
the side of the house with the pressure; he could break
a window with the hammering stream of water; or the
recoil from the spray could hurtle him backwards off
the scaffolding that he has built around the house and
catapult him into the bushes below. I was relieved to
find Bill working behind the garage, not sprawled
across the shrubbery. That water hose, it turns out, is a
wonder. It is one of the best things that has happened
for painters.

New hi-tech tools seem to abound, making many jobs
easier and more precise. They give us the gifts of extra
time and less frustration. Like Bill, I, too, have been ec-
static over new devices that make my quilting even more
joyful. I am astonished at how many new inventions I
have come to rely on and think of as everyday and ordinary. Take, for instance, the rotary cutter. That little

– – – –

razor-sharp rolling wheel has revolutionized the way I make quilts. It, along with some simple, heavy-duty clear plastic rulers, lets me make perfect multi-layered cuts and helps speed my way to the actual sewing stage.

The development of knife-edged scissors is another giant step for all of us. However much we treasure the old scissors in our sewing baskets, they are not nearly as super-keen as our scissors today. When I cut out the pieces for my pine tree quilt a few years back, I had to cut one triangle at a time. Then I got my precious, gleaming new pair of super-sharp scissors, and my old scissors were relegated to cutting paper.

My handy compact quilt frame, too, is a gem. It is a convenient size and folds up neatly when I'm not using it. My faithful older frame was made with the great, long, wooden rails that were held together with C-clamps and needed to be propped up on skinny saw-horses. I had to empty the dining room of furniture to make space for it. With this new frame, I can move from beside the sunny window of my workroom through the door and into the living room at night to enjoy the TV while I quilt.

I sewed on the same old Model T sewing machine for almost 50 years. As sweet is that little machine was, the computer-driven mechanical miracle that I use now sends me into rapture with its tempting fancy stitches, two lights for illumination, and an array of options. Its best pleasures are the simple conveniences. I like the

– – – –

way it effortlessly and evenly feeds the multiple layers of my quilts through beneath the presser foot, the choice I have of whether my needle will come to a stop either up or down, the precision width of the seams, and the choice of motor speeds. I love this sewing machine.

Here, however, is a quandary for you: I can plug in, clean off, oil up, and store away my new tools with the best of you. I cherish these innovations, but I am mentally challenged and emotionally staggered when I venture out into the brave new world of computers. Computers, in general, scare me. While I appreciate that a computer is a valid tool for the quiltmaker, I am intimidated by any equipment that is brighter than I am.

Quilters design on their computers, chat with other quilters around the world on their computers, research on their computers, and sort out the various components of their lives and store them on their computers. In other words, a computer is a multi-use blessing for contemporary quilters. I realize that I am handicapped because I feel threatened by them, but bit by bit, I am coming to terms with my insecurities. One wonderful day, when I have gained enough confidence and I have become electronically well-adjusted, I, too, will become a cyber-quilter.

Moral: Consider the lilies of the field: they toil not, neither do they spin or quilt, but if they had computers, they would most certainly bring forth marvelous things.

– – – –

THE WINDS OF WAS

THE MATERIALS LIST FOR THE WORKSHOP THAT I AM going to take calls for four Log Cabin blocks, already pieced from solid-color fabrics, and suggests several possible color combinations. I've decided to use greens and roses arranged around an off-white center square. My next challenge is to choose five gradations of those colors.

My solid fabrics are stored on floor-to-ceiling shelves in a closet. A few extra fabrics in boxes are stuck on top of a basement bookcase, and I have shoved some bundles of material between the storage boxes under my work table. Scraps of fabric in baggies are tucked into baskets and under piles of fabric waiting for future projects. So much fabric is stashed around this house that to haul out any of it takes a good deal of muscle.

This morning I began pulling out my solid stash from its various caches, one color at a time. I tipped the fabrics out of the assorted boxes and bins and spilled them across the floor. Having discovered long ago that I enjoy using printed fabrics, it's been years since I have used solids. But I still have solids. I learned early on that a quilter is never supposed to waste even the tiniest bits of material.

Packed away are the tag ends of projects, "just in case" I needed one more wee piece of something to finish a quilt. Also tucked away are fabrics full of holes

– – – –

like Swiss cheese, because I precision-cut out little pieces of the designs. And there are pieces of leftover bias because I cut far more than I needed to bind off my quilts. I save everything, because more than once, on a bitter day, I have found myself out in the alley, rummaging through the trash for a discarded selvedge or a scrap of fabric to do a last minute fix-up.

Back in the early '70s, textile manufacturers produced brilliantly colored polyester blends for the American dressmaker. At fabric stores then, quiltmakers would find rows and rows of this shiny, wrinkle-resistant material that slithered when you tried to sew it. But as it was basically the only fabric available, I bought it in great quantities.

This morning, as I looked over what I'd dumped out onto the floor, whole lengths of solids lay about. I found half-yard lengths, sometimes a full yard, and frequently I found 10 or 15 yards, fabrics that have been buried for nearly 30 years. I decided to set up a test station at the kitchen sink. I opened the window for ventilation, and put out a pair of scissors to snip off chunks of material, a pair of tongs to hold the snippets of fabric, a box of matches to light the fabric, and a bowl of water to douse the flame quickly. Quickly and carefully I put a match to each piece of fabric of questionable fiber content, let it flame a moment, dipped it into the water and fingered the burnt edge to discover if the residue was a soft cottony ash, or a hard, polyester curl. I sorted

– – – –

out the polyester blends because I will never, ever, use them again. I folded the large pieces of blends and packed them into paper bags for the local church women who use large squares of these fabrics to make tied comforters for their mission project.

I sorted through the rest of the rubble and laid out every reasonable piece of cotton fabric. I trimmed away threads and scrappy bits and sorted them into hues and tones, piling them in layers so that I could see if I need to fill in a special shade of turquoise or gold. I made trip after trip to the trash container in the alley.

I am overcome with the self-righteous glory of being neat. I have my closet in order with the bins neatly filed, labeled, and lined up on their shelves. All of my fabrics are accessible again, and I have found five lovely shades of rose and five vibrant shades of green for my Log Cabin blocks.

That enormous can in the alley is filled to the lid with a rainbow of colors—tidbits of green, threads of gold, scraps of purple, red, and blue. Tomorrow, city workers will wheel my trash bin tip to the back of their garbage truck and spill my rainbow of fabric into the maw of their vehicle. They will drive to the landfill and take their mobile garbage monster out into the middle of the dump. With a whining of the lift mechanism, they will raise one end of their truck and spill out my fabric into the sunshine and the wind, and my bits and pieces will flutter and drift on the currents of air like

– – – –

jeweled butterflies. They will catch in the breezes and sparkle in the light, and they will transform that dump into a fabric fairyland. And that is good.

– – – –

I AM VENUS

IF I HAD LIVED TWO THOUSAND YEARS AGO, I WOULD have been gorgeous. I have the solid hips and thick waist of the Venus de Milo. None of the slenderness of the modern movie goddesses is mine. My body is dimpled and rippled here and there with good, honest "me." I am demure enough that I will not admit to being slightly overweight or to be suffering from lack of weight control. No, I am merely two thousand years behind the times.

Do you know what that means to a quilter? Whenever I go to quilt meetings where younger quilters appear dressed in quilted vests, pieced jackets, and stenciled and appliquéd skirts and blouses, I pay attention. I say to myself, "There I go." Once home, I shuffle through my pile of patterns and I take out those colored markers that quilters seem to collect. (I have an enormous supply, most of them dried up.) I trace the picture off the front of the pattern envelope and then I sketch.

Since I have collected some great books on imaginative pieced clothing, I know all of the dos and don'ts. I play with all sorts of designs and I know better than to put a broad stripe right around my bustline or to place a couple of pinwheels in embarrassing places on the front of a blouse. I know that quilted garments make a person look heavier. My books tell me that a

– – – –

long vest, ending right at my hips, will make me look elephantine from the back view. I have read about all of these problems, and I try to avoid them.

So, there I sit with my papers and markers, drawing things. The next step is to go to my fabric stash. One advantage to making pieced clothing is that you can use up all those little scraps that you have saved for years in case you might use them someday. Well, *now* is Someday.

I sew for other people fairly well, but I find that sewing for myself is not so easy. Marking my hems and fitting my back views are the hardest. To help myself with these chores, I once bought a dress form at the Goodwill Store for $1.50. It was in its primitive state, all bare bones. I covered it with black t-shirt material and called it my Black Maria. Maria is not as easy to use as I had expected and so she has been relegated to the corner of my workroom where she stands holding pieces of quilt binding over her shoulders.

I have tried hem-marking devices and they are tedious. When I have asked my husband to mark my hems, I have had to stand on the kitchen table with my head touching the ceiling, then turn slowly around. It has been disconcerting to him to discover that the place where he started marking was around an inch and a half lower than the place where he finished. I have finally come to terms with hems. I simply make them exactly the level and length that is indicated on the pattern, and then I never, never look in the mirror. If my husband struggles with hemlines, how could I possibly ask him to tackle bust darts or hip corrections?

All of this is to say that I do not find dressmaking for myself easy. It also says that I plan what I am going to sew very carefully because I know that I will be investing a lot of emotion in the construction of the garment. Armed with all of this self-knowledge and going into the project well prepared, why is it that every piece of clothing I make harbors surprises?

I made myself a skirt that I call Blue Blazes. It is white, and I carefully placed four blazing stars around its flare. I knew that if I put the center of the highest star on my hip, it would look like a bulls-eye. I moved it down a bit. I snipped. I stitched, and I hemmed. Finished at last, I tried it on. The blazing star did not make a bulls-eye on my hip. What did happen was that in lowering the star, its top points cradled my hip and the white background fabric looked like a balloon below my waistband. I removed the waistband, cut two inches off the top of the skirt, gathered it in, and reattached it. I have not looked at the hemline in the mirror. It may or may not be even.

I shall go on being tempted into making clothing for myself. When I go to a style show, sleek women will parade before me draped in slender dresses, showing me their chic, thin selves. I will imagine myself in those elegant dresses. I will go on, too, looking at clever young women at quilt meetings and imagining myself in their pieced clothing. I know that if I put special patchwork touches in my "good" areas they will complement my figure. I have yet to discover exactly where my "good" areas are.

In the meantime, I will remind myself that Venus was beautiful. She represented grace and beauty. Artists have glorified her for centuries. I am Venus.

— — — —

TENDERFOOT

WHEN I WAS A CHILD, I COULD WALK BAREFOOT ACROSS the gnarly oyster-shell roads of Maryland on a hot summer day. Now that I am older, a spilled cornflake on my kitchen floor is rough beneath my feet.

When I was a child, I could ride my bicycle joyously down country roads with the wind rushing up my sleeves and billowing through my blouse. Now, I drive my car to the grocery store two blocks down the street.

When I was a child, I could twirl and twirl in the night until I fell laughing into the grass and the fireflies blinked their fairy signals in the darkness around me. Now, I have to put on my glasses in the broad daylight so that I can see better.

But...

When I was a child, I pulled the bed covers up around me at night, snuggling under them contentedly as I slipped into sleep. Now older, I make quilts for comforting, and I am content.

When I was a child, I played Kick the Can and Hide and Seek with my friends in the soft summer twilight. Those friendships stitched my days together. Now, I treasure the moments I spend sitting at a quilt frame with other quilters. Laughing chatter weaves together confidences and concerns.

When I was a child, I did not count the hours. I woke in the morning and dallied through the day, spending time

- - - -

as if my temporal bank account was endless. Now I find that I panic as time whizzes by. There are never enough moments. I have so much I want to do, and I know that there are only 24 hours on my daily statement.

When I was a child, if I got a sliver in my hand, my father would pick it out gently and my mother would kiss it and make it well. Now, I prick my fingers over and over, quickly putting them in my mouth so that the drops of blood will not stain my quilt. Pricked fingers are a badge of honor among quilters, something of which to be proud.

When I was a child, I ate peanut butter toast because I thought it was delicious. I still eat peanut butter toast, but now I eat it because peanut butter is quick and easy, and it requires almost nothing of me and does not distract me as I stitch.

When I was a child, I dreamed, and so I dream today. From these dreams come the triangles and the diamonds and the squares that form the patterns of my quilts like splintered glass in a kaleidoscope, blossoming out in fractured colors.

When I was a child, I could walk barefoot, unaware, over the hot oyster-shell roads of Maryland. Now, I am grown, and I have learned to be happy with the simple pleasures of damp grass between my shoeless toes.

I am no longer complacent. I have learned to treasure friends and to cherish time, those bits of minutes that we spend pricking our fingers as we stitch out our

— — — —

visions. I have not grown away from childhood dalliances. Being older, I have only transformed them. Quilting is such a simple, barefoot joy.

ABOUT THE AUTHOR

HELEN KELLEY IS A QUILTMAKER, LECTURER, AUTHOR, and instructor based in Minneapolis, Minnesota. Since she bought her first sewing machine—a Singer Featherweight—in 1946, she has made more than 115 quilts and wall hangings, many of which are of masterpiece quality and have been displayed at shows both nationally and internationally.

Widely respected by the quilting community, Helen was the first president of the Minnesota Quilter's Guild and has received an abundance of awards for her quilts. In 1999, at the International Quilt Festival in Houston, Texas, her "Renaissance Quilt" was chosen as one of the 100 Best American Quilts of the Twentieth Century.

Helen's "Loose Threads" articles have appeared monthly in *Quilter's Newsletter Magazine* for twenty years. Written in wry and pertinent language, the column has long been a favorite of readers. Helen is the author of the best-selling book *Every Quilt Tells a Story: A Quilter's Stash of Wit and Wisdom,* also published by Voyageur Press. Her other books include *Scarlet Ribbons: American Indian Technique for Today's Quilters*; *Dating Quilts: From 1600 to the Present*; and two self-published books of flower patterns. She was also featured in Oxmoor House's *Quilt with the Best.* In addition, Helen's by-line has appeared in a variety of quilting publications, and her prize-winning quilts have been the subject of numerous photo essays.

– – – –